Caprial
Cooks for Friends

Caprial

Cooks for Friends

CAPRIAL PENCE

Photography by PAUL YONCHEK
Food Styling by HEATHER BOWEN

TEN SPEED PRESS
Berkeley   Toronto

1⊜

Ten Speed Press
P.O. Box 7123
Berkeley, California 94707
www.tenspeed.com

Distributed in Australia by Simon and Schuster
Australia, in Canada by Ten Speed Press Canada, in
New Zealand by Southern Publishers Group, in South
Africa by Real Books, in Southeast Asia by Berkeley
Books, and in the United Kingdom and Europe by
Airlift Books.

Design by Toni Tajima
Writing Assistance by Jennifer Morrison,
     Portland, Oregon
Food Photography by Paul Yonchek, Portland, Oregon
Food Styling by Heather Bowen, Portland, Oregon,
     with assistance from Lisa Lanxon
Special thanks to Carl Greve who kindly loaned props
Produced in association with Culinary Arts Television,
     Tiburon, CA

Library of Congress Cataloging-in-Publication Data
Pence, Caprial
     Caprial cooks for friends/by Caprial Pence;
photography by Paul Yonchek; food styling by
Heather Bowen.
          p. cm.
     Includes index.
     ISBN 1-58008-152-5 (cloth)
     1. Cookery, American—Pacific Northwest style.
I. Title.
TX715.2.P32 P4596 2000
641.5979—dc21   99-086283

First printing, 2000
Printed in Canada

1 2 3 4 5 6 7 8 9 10 — 04 03 02 01 00

To my mom, Artheen, who makes
the world's best pork chops

Love, Cappy

contents

Acknowledgments viii

A Note on Using This Book ix

Introduction 1

1 / Appetizers and Sides 4

2 / Salads and Soups 50

3 / Entrées 68

4 / Vegetarian Entrées 120

5 / Desserts 148

Basics 184

Glossary 191

Menus 193

Index 195

Entertaining Primers

• Cocktails / 16

• Essentials for a Well-Stocked Bar / 28

• Cheese / 40

• Entertaining off the Cuff / 58

• How Much Should I Make? / 82

• Tips for Serving Wine / 98

• Five Drinks without the Fire but with
    All the Sizzle / 112

• When to Call for Help / 131

• Centerpieces / 145

• Other Things to Worry about Besides
    the Menu / 173

Acknowledgments

Thanks to Jane MacQueen, Steve Shapiro, and Wendy Sheldon who kindly allowed the use of their homes for the photographs.

Thanks to Carl Greve for the use of props, china, and glassware for the photographs.

Thanks to Lisa Lanxon, Heather Bowen, and Paul Yonchek for all their hard work and effort.

Thanks to the Bistro staff for answering all the questions and for all their hard work.

A Great Big Thanks to Jenny Morrison for helping to make my life easier and my books better.

Thanks to Toni Tajima, Aaron Wehner, and Lorena Jones at Ten Speed for all your work and support.

Thanks to my family and friends for all their support and love.

A Note on Using This Book

Convection ovens are becoming increasingly popular in home kitchens. Many people are confused by convection cooking, assuming that it is either just like cooking with a standard oven or that it is very complicated. Basically, a convection oven works by heating air and circulating it throughout the oven, which helps cook things faster, more evenly, and at a lower temperature than a standard oven. Convection cooking works especially well for baking and roasting. A holiday turkey, for example, will cook in three hours instead of the standard six, coming out golden brown and crispy on the outside and juicy on the inside. And for blind baking (pre-baking) tart shells, a convection oven is very effective, setting the pastry so quickly that the crust doesn't have time to soften, shrink, and slump. It's hard to beat the browning results of a convection oven, but to bake more delicate items like crème brûlée and crème caramel, it's better to use the standard mode.

For successful convection cooking, you'll need to make adjustments to a recipe's cooking temperature and time to ensure the finished dish doesn't come out nicely browned on the outside but undercooked on the inside. As a rule of thumb, reduce the oven temperature called for by 25 percent. (When the specified cooking time is less than 30 minutes, usually no adjustment is necessary.) For example, to cook the Crown Roast with Roasted Pear and Walnut Dressing (page 107) in a standard oven, you should first roast it at 425° for 15 minutes, then at 350° for about 1¹/₂ hours. Adjusted for a convection oven, the breakdown should be 400° for 15 minutes, then 325° for about 1 hour. Either way, be sure to cook the roast until it reaches an internal temperature of 145°. (Roasting times of meat and poultry will vary according to the size, shape, and quality of the product.) By making these simple adjustments in cooking time and temperature, you'll be using your convection oven to its fullest potential.

introductio

Years ago, someone told me that if I really wanted to start a restaurant, I'd better love to entertain. After eight years of running my own restaurant with my husband, John, I couldn't agree more. While the food is the center of attention at the Bistro, it's just as important for us to be good hosts. This means doing anything to make our guests comfortable and to help them really enjoy themselves. Fortunately, like most people who enjoy cooking, we love to share it with others. Cooking is our profession, but it is also an important part of our lives, a significant way that we express who we are. It's no wonder we love to entertain at home. Even if we've been busy cooking at the restaurant, we always look forward to dreaming up a menu, shopping for just the right ingredients, preparing the meal, and welcoming family and friends into our home for our next gathering.

The tradition of entertaining probably began when people gathered together to celebrate important cultural events and religious rituals—families joining together for a marriage feast, to honor the birth of a baby, or to celebrate the harvest. Things are no different today: Important moments naturally call for gathering around a tasty array of food and toasting the occasion with a good bottle of wine. For many people, having extended family over for a birthday party or for Thanksgiving dinner may be the only time they entertain all year. While John and I like to have people over during the holidays, it can be such a busy, stressful time at the restaurant that trying to enjoy a party at home can be rather challenging. So instead, we like to entertain when we can really relax and enjoy our company and the evening. More often than not, there isn't a special occasion—dinner with friends just sounded like a good idea. For me, entertaining isn't only about well-planned, elaborate, multi-course, sit-down affairs. Although it's certainly fun to pull out all the stops, a low-key get-together for barbecued ribs on a Sunday afternoon or even an impromptu evening of conversation with a friend over a quick seafood frittata ranks just as high on my list.

Whatever the definition of entertaining that fits the moment at hand, I want to be able to spend time with my guests rather than be stuck in the kitchen all evening—and no doubt you feel the same. The people and the time you spend with them are the heart of any good party, and as the host, you need to be a part of the occasion. After all, if you can't enjoy the fun, what's the point? Think of the difference between grilling a piece of meat and hosting a barbecue. Grilling might be nothing more memorable than cooking your dinner, but a barbecue is an event, an occasion. I hear the word "barbecue" and envision kicking back with good friends on a balmy evening, the inviting aromas of chicken and ribs cooking on the grill, the sound of kids playing on the lawn, and the taste of a smooth Zinfandel or a cold beer. I want this book to help you create memorable events, so you can savor the time you spend with your own family and friends.

What's the secret to successful entertaining? It definitely is *not* having a large, beautiful kitchen. You may be thinking that that's easy for me to say, as you envision me cooking at home in a modern, spacious chef's dream kitchen. Actually, I speak from experience: John and I have been in the same house, which was built in 1927, for five years, and we have yet to face the remodel of its original and diminutive kitchen, which has one short counter—and no dishwasher. We do have sharp knives, a gas stove, and a food processor, but that's about it for amenities. Our training and experience as professional chefs have taught us how to organize and plan, which is the key to alleviating the pressure and smoothly orchestrating any great dinner party. As long as you think ahead about your menu and are prepared to pull it off, there's no reason to be intimidated by hosting any type of party in your own home.

You may be the kind of person for whom being a host is second nature. If everyone naturally gravitates toward your house, I hope you'll find new and useful ideas in this book, giving you even more reasons to throw a party. On the other hand, if you don't entertain very often, I'd be thrilled if this book inspired you to share your cooking with other people. Along with recipes for every course, you'll find several menus for different types of gatherings. To help you save time, I share my tips on steps you can take that will help you prepare dishes ahead of time.

After you've put time and effort into cooking a wonderful meal, you'll want to give some thought to the presentation of each dish. Since first impressions do count, I offer garnishing and serving ideas that will help add visual impact. I've also suggested a wine that I feel makes a good match with each entrée—but I don't get more particular than the type or particular varietal of wine, to give you more flexibility in cost, vintner, and personal preference.

Of course, there's even more to successful entertaining than planning ahead, preparing delicious recipes, and choosing just the right wines to serve. As John and I have been enthusiastically hosting over the years, experience has shown us all kinds of things that can really enhance a dinner party and even affect how enjoyable it will be for guests. Sometimes it's a rather embarrassing oversight that teaches a lesson, like the time we forgot to count chairs. It was one of the first dinner parties we threw together, and we had six guests, but only four people could sit down! Even now we are constantly adding to our mental list of lessons learned. To help you entertain with ease, I've included other tried-and-true advice and useful information, from how to make great drinks to suggestions on how to keep a well-stocked pantry for last-minute parties.

Whether you're serving beef tenderloin or chili, when you get right down to it, what matters most is that you extend the invitation. I hope you'll get enthused about making opportunities for entertaining. Once you throw your first successful dinner party, you'll be encouraged and have the confidence to do it again and again. No longer will you think of entertaining as a chore, but as something to look forward to.

appetizers and sides

Tomato-Basil Tart / 6

Tuna Tartare with Wasabi Vinaigrette / 7

Mini Pizza Turnovers / 8

Fava Bean Bruschetta / 9

One-Minute Salmon with Lemongrass-Soy
    Aioli / 10

Flank Steak Satay with Curry Dipping
    Sauce / 11

Sautéed Butternut Squash with Lime-
    Coconut Sauce / 12

Wild Mushroom Tarte Tatin / 13

Marinated Melon Wedges / 14

Potato Pancakes with Smoked Salmon
    Salad / 15

Baked Tortilla Chips with Two Salsas / 18

Pan-Fried Seafood Sausage / 20

Zucchini Gratin / 21

Sesame-Cheddar Crackers / 22

Shiitake Spring Rolls / 23

Mark's Jungle Rice / 24

Chilled Five-Spice Prawns with Caper
    Aioli / 25

Green Onion—Buttermilk Biscuits / 26

Creamy Garlic Spinach / 27

Smoked Salmon Pizza / 30

Socca / 31

Eggplant and Blue Cheese Spread / 32

Poblano Chile Dip / 33

Sautéed Baby Bok Choy with Toasted Sesame
    Sauce / 34

Orange-Chile Noodles / 35

Dad's Baked Beans / 36

John's Fried Corn / 37

Clams with Hot-and-Sour Sauce / 38

Bread Salad / 39

Roasted Baby New Potatoes with Olive
    Tapenade / 41

Steamed Cauliflower with Sundried
    Tomatoes and Roasted Garlic / 42

The Best Mashed Potatoes / 43

French Fries / 44

Oven Home Fries / 45

Marinated Sweet Peppers / 46

Marinated Olives / 47

Deep-Fried Prawns with Three-Onion
    Chutney / 48

TOMATO-BASIL TART

I specify vine-ripened tomatoes in this recipe because the success of this dish depends more on the ripeness than the type of tomatoes you use. I started making this tart to take along whenever we went on a picnic; everyone liked it so much that I now serve it as a starter for summer dinner parties or as part of a brunch.

Roasted Garlic Crust

2 cups flour
1 head roasted garlic (page 185)
Pinch salt
1 cup unsalted butter, diced

Tomato-Basil Filling

³/₄ cup freshly grated Parmesan cheese
1 cup chopped fresh basil
12 ounces soft, mild goat cheese
1 teaspoon chopped fresh Italian parsley
4 eggs
Salt
Freshly cracked black pepper
8 vine-ripened tomatoes, thinly sliced

To prepare the crust: Preheat the oven to 350°. Place the flour, roasted garlic, and salt in the bowl of a food processor. With the motor running, add the butter, a few pieces at a time, through the feed tube, and process until a dough forms on top of the blades. Press the dough into a well-greased 10-inch flan or tart pan with a removable bottom. Bake just until the crust is set, about 10 minutes. Let cool completely.

To prepare the filling: Sprinkle about ¹/₂ cup of the Parmesan cheese over the bottom of the crust, and then sprinkle the basil over it. In a small bowl, combine the goat cheese, parsley, and eggs, and mix well. Season with salt and pepper. Spread the goat cheese mixture over the basil. Arrange the tomatoes on top, and sprinkle with the remaining Parmesan cheese. Bake just until the cheese is golden brown, about 30 minutes. Let cool 15 to 20 minutes. Serve at room temperature.

TUNA TARTARE with WASABI VINAIGRETTE

SERVES 6

The adventuresome guests in your gathering will love this appetizer's bright flavors. For even more impact, serve it on oversized square white plates to show off the dramatic presentation and beautiful contrasting colors.

Wasabi Vinaigrette

3 tablespoons rice vinegar

1 tablespoon wasabi paste

1 clove garlic, chopped

1 teaspoon peeled, chopped fresh ginger

$1/2$ cup vegetable oil

2 teaspoons sesame oil

$1/2$ teaspoon chile paste

Soy sauce

Tuna Tartare

12 ounces extremely fresh ahi tuna, minced

2 cloves garlic, minced

2 teaspoons peeled, chopped fresh ginger

2 teaspoons chopped fresh cilantro

Grated zest and juice of 1 lime

2 teaspoons soy sauce

$1/2$ teaspoon chile paste

6 very large spinach leaves, rinsed and spun dry

12 chives, blanched and sliced (page 188)

$1/4$ cup pickled ginger, for garnish (available at specialty grocery stores)

To prepare the vinaigrette: In a bowl, whisk together the vinegar, wasabi paste, garlic, and ginger. While whisking, slowly add the vegetable oil, and whisk until smooth and emulsified. Add the sesame oil, chile paste, and soy sauce, and whisk well. Set aside. (The vinaigrette can be made in advance and kept refrigerated for up to 1 week.)

To prepare the tuna tartare: In a bowl, combine the tuna, garlic, ginger, cilantro, lime zest and juice, and chile paste, and mix well. Season with the soy sauce to taste.

To assemble: Place 1 spinach leaf on a flat work surface with the stem end pointing toward you. Place about $1/4$ cup of the tuna mixture on the center of the spinach leaf. Roll up the spinach leaf. Secure the roll with 2 chives, tying one about $1/4$ inch from each edge. Repeat with the remaining leaves, tuna mixture, and chives.

To serve: Using a very sharp serrated knife, cut each roll in half on the diagonal. Place 2 halves, cut side down, on each plate. Drizzle with the vinaigrette, and garnish with pickled ginger. Serve immediately.

MINI PIZZA TURNOVERS

These may not be the kind of appetizers you'd expect to see in one of my books. But served as part of the child's birthday party menu (see page 193), these cheesy turnovers are right at home with the corn dogs and chocolate cake. I bet you'll see more than one adult snitching a few!

$1/2$ **recipe puff pastry (page 190)**
2 cups tomato sauce (page 188)
2 ounces thinly sliced salami, julienned
$3/4$ **cup grated mozzarella cheese**
$1/3$ **cup freshly grated Parmesan cheese**
$1/3$ **cup chopped black olives**

Preheat the oven to 375°. On a well-floured board, roll the puff pastry dough out into a 24 by 8-inch rectangle, then cut it into twelve 4-inch squares. Place about 1 teaspoon of the tomato sauce in the center of each square, then top with the salami, mozzarella, Parmesan, and olives, dividing them equally. Lightly brush the edges of the dough with water. Fold one corner of each square over to form a triangle, and seal the edges with a fork. Place the turnovers on a greased baking sheet, and bake until golden brown, about 20 minutes. Let cool for 10 minutes before serving, or until tepid.

To serve, place the turnovers on a platter, and serve the remaining tomato sauce on the side for dipping.

FAVA BEAN BRUSCHETTA

SERVES 8

Bruschetta really is best served warm, but doing so can make things a bit hectic if you're trying to greet your guests at the door, pour the wine, and work on the final touches of the entrée. Luckily, you can prepare all elements of this appetizer well before the doorbell starts ringing. Make the spread up to a week in advance, and get the toppings ready up to two hours ahead—then all you have to do is top the bread once it's toasted and warm. I also like to serve the fava bean spread on sandwiches, such as grilled chicken, or even on seared salmon.

Fava Bean Spread

$1/2$ cup dried fava beans

Zest and juice of 1 lemon

2 cloves garlic, chopped

$1/3$ cup extra virgin olive oil

1 tablespoon chopped fresh basil

Salt

Freshly ground black pepper

1 baguette, sliced on the diagonal into $1/4$-inch-
   thick slices

$1/4$ cup extra virgin olive oil

4 ounces thinly sliced prosciutto, julienned

2 ounces arugula, rinsed and spun dry

$1/2$ cup freshly grated Parmesan cheese

To prepare the fava bean spread: Place the fava beans in a saucepan and add enough cold water to cover. Simmer over medium heat until tender, adding additional water as needed. Combine the fava beans, lemon zest and juice, and garlic in the bowl of a food processor and process until smooth. With the motor running, slowly add the olive oil through the feed tube and process until smooth. Add the basil and process to mix. Season to taste with salt and pepper. Set aside or refrigerate for up to 1 week.

To prepare the bruschetta: Preheat the oven to 350°. Place the baguette slices on a baking sheet and brush with about 2 tablespoons of the olive oil. Bake until toasted and golden brown, about 15 minutes. Remove the toasts from the oven and spread each with the fava bean mixture. Distribute the prosciutto among the toasts, then top with the arugula and Parmesan cheese. Just before serving, drizzle with the remaining 2 tablespoons olive oil.

ONE-MINUTE SALMON with LEMONGRASS-SOY AIOLI

SERVES 6

This beautiful appetizer makes a perfect beginning for an elegant evening. It literally takes about one minute to cook, so I suggest you have the aioli ready, everyone seated at the table, and the wine poured before you even start to cook the salmon.

Lemongrass-Soy Aioli

2 teaspoons peeled, chopped fresh ginger

1 clove garlic, chopped

1 stalk lemongrass, finely minced

Juice of $^1/_2$ lemon

1 egg yolk

1 cup vegetable oil

Pinch dried red chile flakes

Soy sauce

1 tablespoon unsalted butter

1 (2-pound) salmon fillet

$^1/_4$ cup pickled ginger, for garnish (available at specialty grocery stores)

To prepare the aioli: Place the ginger, garlic, lemongrass, lemon juice, and egg yolk in a food processor and purée. With the machine running, slowly add the vegetable oil through the feed tube and process until very thick and emulsified. Add the chile flakes and season to taste with soy sauce. Process again briefly to mix. Refrigerate until ready to serve, or up to 1 week.

To prepare the salmon: Preheat the oven to 425°. Butter six 6-inch ovenproof plates. Using an extremely sharp knife, slice the fillet crosswise into $^1/_8$-inch-thick pieces. Place 3 slices in a single layer on each plate, covering the whole plate with the salmon. Set the plates in the oven and cook for 1 to 2 minutes, or until the salmon starts to turn light pink. Drizzle the salmon with aioli, top with pickled ginger, and serve immediately.

NOTE: Children and individuals who are immunosuppressed should not eat uncooked eggs that have not been pasteurized.

FLANK STEAK SATAY with CURRY DIPPING SAUCE

MAKES 16 TO 20 SKEWERS

I like to serve this appetizer when I'm having a large party. I skewer the steak and prepare the dipping sauce in advance. Then, as my guests arrive, I grill just enough of the steak so they can savor it while it's hot.

Curry Dipping Sauce

1 tablespoon curry powder, toasted (page 186)

2 tablespoons rice vinegar

2 cloves garlic, chopped

2 teaspoons peeled, chopped fresh ginger

$1/2$ cup coconut milk

$1/3$ cup vegetable oil

Grated zest and juice of 1 lime

Soy sauce

Flank Steak Satay

2 pounds flank steak, sliced thinly against the grain

1 tablespoon five-spice powder

1 teaspoon brown sugar

1 teaspoon curry powder, toasted (page 186)

1 teaspoon ground cumin, toasted (page 186)

Salt

To prepare the dipping sauce: In a small bowl, whisk together the curry powder, vinegar, garlic, ginger, and coconut milk until smooth. While whisking, slowly add the vegetable oil and whisk until thick and emulsified. Whisk in the lime zest and juice. Season to taste with soy sauce. Set aside. (The sauce can be prepared in advance and kept refrigerated for up to 1 week.)

To prepare the satay: Oil the grill and heat until very hot. (To test, you should be able to hold your hand over the grill for no more than 5 seconds.) Meanwhile, soak 16 to 20 bamboo skewers in water for 10 minutes. Place each slice of steak on a skewer. In a small bowl, combine the five-spice powder, brown sugar, curry powder, and cumin, and mix well. Rub the steak with the spice mixture.

Season the skewered steak with salt, and then place on the grill and cook on each side for 3 minutes. Serve warm, with the dipping sauce on the side.

SAUTÉED BUTTERNUT SQUASH with LIME-COCONUT SAUCE

SERVES 4

This has everything a memorable side dish needs—complexity, intense flavor, and rich color. For a change of flavor and texture, try adding more tender vegetables, such as baby bok choy, toward the end of the cooking time.

2 tablespoons vegetable oil

1 large butternut squash, peeled and cut into
　　large dice

2 cloves garlic, chopped

2 teaspoons peeled, chopped fresh ginger

$^1/_2$ cup dry white wine

$^1/_4$ cup honey

$^1/_2$ cup roasted vegetable stock (page188)

2 (12-ounce) cans coconut milk

Grated zest and juice of 1 lime

1 teaspoon curry powder, toasted (page 186)

1 tablespoon chopped fresh basil

2 teaspoons chile sauce

Soy sauce

$^1/_2$ cup toasted fresh coconut, for garnish

$^1/_2$ cup fried shallots (page 185), for garnish

Heat the oil in a very large sauté pan over high heat until smoking hot. Add the squash and sear, without stirring, for 3 to 4 minutes. Toss and sear, without stirring, 3 to 4 minutes longer. Add the garlic and ginger, and sauté for 1 minute. Add the wine and honey and cook until reduced by one-half, about 4 minutes. Add the stock and coconut milk, lower the heat to medium, and simmer just until the squash is tender, about 10 minutes. Stir in the lime zest and juice, curry powder, basil, and chile sauce. Season with soy sauce to taste. Serve warm, sprinkled with toasted coconut and fried shallots.

WILD MUSHROOM TARTE TATIN

SERVES 10

When I created this take on tarte Tatin, I was torn between cutting it into small wedges and calling it an appetizer and serving larger pieces with a salad and wine and calling it an entrée—it's that versatile. No matter what you call it, you'll want to add it to your entertaining repertoire. If wild mushrooms are not in season, use domestic mushrooms along with reconstituted dried wild mushrooms.

Parmesan Crust

1¹/₃ cups flour

1 teaspoon salt

¹/₂ cup finely grated Parmesan cheese

¹/₄ cup shortening

¹/₄ cup unsalted butter, diced

6 tablespoons cold water

Wild Mushroom Filling

1 tablespoon unsalted butter

2 cloves garlic, chopped

1 shallot, chopped

3 cups sliced seasonal wild mushrooms

¹/₂ cup balsamic vinegar

1 teaspoon chopped fresh thyme

1 teaspoon chopped fresh basil

1 teaspoon chopped fresh rosemary

Salt

Freshly ground black pepper

4 ounces soft, mild goat cheese

To prepare the crust: Combine the flour, salt, and Parmesan in a bowl. Add the shortening and butter. Using your fingertips, mix just until the mixture resembles a coarse meal. Add the water and mix with a fork until the dough just comes together. Roll it into a ball, wrap tightly in plastic wrap, and let rest for 15 to 30 minutes. (The dough can be prepared in advance and kept refrigerated for up to 4 days, or frozen for up to 6 months.)

To prepare the filling: Preheat the oven to 425°. Melt the butter in an ovenproof 10-inch non-stick sauté pan over high heat. Add the garlic and shallot and sauté for 2 minutes. Add the mushrooms and sauté for 4 minutes. Add the balsamic vinegar and reduce until very thick and the mushrooms are tender, about 3 minutes. Add the thyme, basil, and rosemary, and toss well. Season to taste with salt and pepper. Crumble the goat cheese over the mushrooms.

To assemble the tarte Tatin: On a well-floured board, roll the dough out into a 12-inch circle, and place it over the mushrooms in the sauté pan. Crimp the edges to seal the dough. Bake until golden brown, about 20 minutes. Remove the tarte Tatin from the oven and let cool for 5 minutes.

To serve: Flip the tarte Tatin over onto a serving plate. Cut into wedges and serve warm.

MARINATED MELON WEDGES

SERVES 6

I make this for Christmas morning breakfast, which is almost more important to me than the dinner. But since I'm not a morning person, I want to be able to prepare as much of the breakfast as I can the night before. If I marinate the melon in advance, it's one less thing I have to prepare in the morning.

1 large, ripe seasonal melon, seeded and cut into
    12 wedges
¹/₂ cup sugar
1 cup Riesling or other sweet white wine
¹/₄ cup orange liqueur
1 large slice peeled, fresh ginger
1 cinnamon stick
1 teaspoon frozen orange juice concentrate, thawed
Dash vanilla extract
1 teaspoon chopped fresh mint
Mint sprigs, for garnish

Place the melon in a high-sided baking dish. In a saucepan over high heat, combine the sugar, wine, liqueur, ginger, cinnamon stick, orange juice concentrate, vanilla, and chopped mint. Bring the mixture to a boil and cook until the sugar has dissolved, about 5 minutes. Let the syrup cool completely, then pour it over the melon. Cover and refrigerate for at least 1 hour, or up to 24 hours.

To serve, place the melon on a platter, pour the marinade over the top, and garnish with mint sprigs. Serve cold.

Illustrated on page 102a

POTATO PANCAKES with SMOKED SALMON SALAD

SERVES 6

This dish is so good that John tells our cooking class students that if their marriage is in trouble, serving these potato pancakes will solve the problem. If these have the power to save a marriage, you can imagine what they'll do for a party!

Smoked Salmon Salad

6 ounces smoked salmon

1 red onion, julienned

2 cloves garlic, chopped

2 green onions, minced

Grated zest and juice of 1 lemon

$1/4$ cup extra virgin olive oil

Salt

Freshly ground black pepper

Potato Pancakes

2 large Yukon Gold potatoes

2 Granny Smith apples, peeled and grated

$1/3$ cup fried shallots (page 185)

2 eggs

$1/2$ cup flour

2 tablespoons chopped fresh chives

Salt

Freshly ground black pepper

$1/4$ cup extra virgin olive oil

$1/2$ cup sour cream, as an accompaniment

To prepare the salad: Break the smoked salmon into pieces and place in a large bowl. Add the onion, garlic, and green onion and gently toss to mix. Add the lemon zest and juice and olive oil, and mix gently. Season to taste with salt and pepper and set aside.

To prepare the pancakes: Place the potatoes in a saucepan over high heat, cover with water, and boil until tender. Drain and let cool. When cool enough to handle, coarsely grate the potatoes (discard any large pieces of potato skin). Combine the grated potatoes, apples, shallots, eggs, flour, and chives in a bowl and mix well. Season with salt and pepper. Heat about half of the olive oil in a large sauté pan over high heat until very hot. Drop heaping tablespoonfuls of the pancake mixture into the hot oil and cook 2 to 3 minutes per side, until golden brown. Drain on paper towels. Repeat with the remaining pancake mixture, adding more oil as necessary.

To serve: Place 2 pancakes on each individual plate. Spoon the salad over the top of the cakes, and garnish with a dollop of sour cream.

Cocktails

Cocktails are as popular now as they were back in the 1950s, so during our much-anticipated expansion of the Bistro in 1998 we included a full bar in the remodel. We've always enjoyed making good cocktails to serve during special gatherings at home, and we wanted the Bistro's bar to reflect the same spirit. When we planned our cocktail menu, it was important that we serve quality, handcrafted drinks. We knew we wanted to make really good versions of the old standards—like gin-and-tonics, martinis, Manhattans, and old-fashioneds—and we had fun putting our own twist on contemporary drinks such as lemon drops and cosmopolitans.

Serving cocktails during a party at home can easily be overwhelming. Since you probably don't want to be a bartender at the helm of a full-service bar, I suggest keeping it to just one or two different types of drinks. And just as you do when preparing a recipe for an appetizer or entrée, use the best ingredients for the very best results. Freshly squeezed juices, fresh fruit, and high-quality liquor will make all the difference.

The following cocktails are very easy to make at home. They require no fancy tools or equipment, except for some basic bar essentials: a shot glass that measures one ounce, a shaker, a muddler (a small wooden implement used to mash fruit, ice, and herbs such as mint), and glasses. Once you've mastered the simple technique of making first-rate drinks, you might find that you are the featured entertainment at your next dinner party—confidently measuring, mixing, pouring, and serving cocktails with flair.

MARTINI

¹/₄ ounce dry vermouth
2 ounces vodka or gin
Olive or a twist of lemon, for garnish

Add the vermouth to a chilled martini glass. Swirl and pour out. Fill a cocktail shaker with ice. Add the vodka and shake or stir. Strain into the chilled glass. Garnish with an olive or a twist of lemon.

LEMON DROP

³/₄ ounce sweet-and-sour mix (page 29)
³/₄ ounce citron vodka
³/₄ ounce triple sec
Twist of lemon for garnish

Sugar the rim of a chilled martini glass. Fill a cocktail shaker with ice. Add the sweet-and-sour mix, and muddle. Add vodka and triple sec. Shake well. Strain into the glass. Garnish with a twist of lemon zest.

COSMOPOLITAN

1 ounce citron vodka

$^1/_2$ ounce triple sec

$^1/_4$ ounce lime juice

$^1/_4$ ounce simple syrup (page 29)

Splash Chambord

Splash cranberry juice

Twist of lime, for garnish

Fill a cocktail shaker with ice. Add all the ingredients. Shake well. Strain into a chilled martini glass. Garnish with a twist of lime.

MARGARITA

Kosher salt, for rim of glass

$^1/_2$ lime, quartered

1 lemon wedge

1 sugar cube

$1^1/_2$ ounces tequila

$^3/_4$ ounce triple sec

Salt the rim of a chilled, tall glass. Fill it with ice. Fill a cocktail shaker with ice. Add the lime, lemon, and sugar cube, and muddle. Add the tequila and triple sec. Shake well. Strain into the glass.

BRAZILIAN

$^1/_2$ lime

1 sugar cube

2 ounces rum

Twist of lime, for garnish

Fill a chilled glass with ice. Add the lime and sugar cube, and muddle. Stir in the rum. Garnish with a twist of lime.

BAKED TORTILLA CHIPS with TWO SALSAS

I like to prepare these tortilla chips when I have a big party because they are homemade but don't involve the mess of frying corn chips. I season them with a simple mixture of kosher salt and chile powder, but you can also use all kinds of spices or chopped fresh herbs. Keep the baked chips stored in an airtight container for up to two days. If you are short on time, you don't have to prepare both salsas—but I like the contrast of the flavors.

Avocado Salsa

3 avocados, peeled and diced

$1/2$ red onion, minced

2 cloves garlic, minced

Zest and juice of 1 orange

$1/2$ teaspoon frozen orange juice concentrate, thawed

2 teaspoons ground cumin, toasted (page 186)

1 teaspoon ground coriander, toasted (page 186)

1 teaspoon chile powder

Salt

Freshly ground black pepper

Tomatillo and Roasted Chile Salsa

2 tablespoons extra virgin olive oil

1 pound tomatillos, husked removed and rinsed

1 onion, diced

2 cloves garlic, chopped

2 tablespoons rice vinegar

2 poblano chiles, roasted, peeled, seeded, and diced (page 186)

2 red bell peppers, roasted, peeled, seeded, and diced (page 186)

2 jalapeños, roasted, peeled, seeded, and diced (page 186)

2 teaspoons cumin, roasted (page 186)

Salt

Freshly ground black pepper

Baked Tortilla Chips

1 dozen flour tortillas, cut into eight wedges each

2 tablespoons extra virgin olive oil

1 tablespoon kosher salt

1 tablespoon chile powder

To prepare the avocado salsa: In a small bowl, combine the avocados, onion, and garlic, and mix well. Add the orange zest and juice, orange juice concentrate, cumin, coriander, and chile powder, and mix well. Season to taste with salt and pepper. Refrigerate until ready to serve, or up to 2 days.

To prepare the tomatillo salsa: Preheat the oven to 425°. Heat the olive oil in a large ovenproof sauté pan over high heat until smoking hot. Add the tomatillos (leave them whole) and sear for 4 to 5 minutes. Place the pan in the oven and cook the tomatillos for 10 minutes. Add the onion and garlic, and cook until the tomatillos are brown and plump, about 10 minutes longer. Transfer the mixture to a food processor and pulse to coarsely chop the tomatillos. Place the tomatillo mixture in a bowl, add the rice vinegar, chiles, peppers, and cumin, and mix well. Season to taste with salt and pepper. Refrigerate until ready to serve, or up to 1 week.

To prepare the tortilla chips: Preheat the oven to 350°. Place the tortilla wedges on a large baking sheet, drizzle with the olive oil, and sprinkle with the kosher salt and chile powder. Bake until golden brown, 10 to 15 minutes. Serve warm or at room temperature, with the salsas on the side.

salsa

PAN-FRIED SEAFOOD SAUSAGE

SERVES 6

I've been making these versatile sausages since I was the chef at Fuller's in Seattle, and they've appeared on many menus and at many parties at home—as an appetizer, entrée, and even as a brunch item. They require some time to prepare, but once they're formed, all they require is a short stint in the sauté pan.

12 ounces sea scallops, diced

8 ounces halibut or other mild whitefish, diced

3 shallots, finely chopped

2 cloves garlic, chopped

1 cup heavy whipping cream

4 large prawns, peeled, deveined, and diced

4 ounces crabmeat

1 teaspoon finely chopped chives

$^{1}/_{2}$ red bell pepper, seeded and cut into small dice

1 teaspoon finely chopped fresh thyme

Salt

Freshly ground black pepper

Flour, for dredging

2 tablespoons extra virgin olive oil

Red Pepper Rouille (page 108), as an accompaniment

To prepare the seafood mousse: Place the bowl and blade of a food processor in the freezer to chill. In the chilled bowl of the food processor, combine the scallops, halibut, shallots, and garlic, and process until smooth. With the motor running, slowly add the cream through the feed tube and process until smooth. Transfer the mousse to a mixing bowl. Fold in the prawns, crab, chives, red bell pepper, and thyme, and season with salt and pepper. Mix well.

To form the sausages: Transfer the mousse to a large pastry bag without a tip. Spread a 50-inch-long piece of plastic wrap out on the counter. Pipe the mousse into about a 48-inch-long strip down the middle of the plastic wrap, stopping at least 1 inch from each end. Fold one side of the plastic wrap over the mousse. Tightly roll up the mousse in the excess plastic wrap. With a piece of butcher's twine, securely tie one end of the roll. About every 5 inches, tie a knot with a piece of twine to form sausages, securing the end of the roll with a knot.

To cook the sausages: Bring about 8 cups of water to a boil in a large stockpot. Add the sausages (they should still be in the plastic wrap) and cook until firm, 6 to 8 minutes. Remove the sausages from the water and let cool for 10 minutes. (The sausages can be prepared up to this point and kept refrigerated for up to 2 days.)

To sauté the sausages: Unwrap the sausages and dredge them in flour. Heat the olive oil in a large sauté pan over high heat until very hot. Add the sausages and brown well, about 3 to 4 minutes. To serve, slice on the diagonal and drizzle with rouille. Serve warm.

ZUCCHINI GRATIN

SERVES 6

This recipe provides a great opportunity for using up fresh zucchini out of the garden. Since you can have it ready to bake ahead of time, it makes a perfect side dish for summer parties and barbecues.

4 zucchini, cut on the diagonal into $\frac{1}{8}$-inch-thick slices
Salt
Freshly ground black pepper
4 thick slices French bread, torn into pieces
2 cloves garlic
2 teaspoons chopped fresh oregano
1 teaspoon chopped fresh rosemary
1 teaspoon Dijon mustard
2 tablespoons extra virgin olive oil

Preheat the oven to 375°. Butter a 2-quart baking dish. Arrange the zucchini slices in concentric circles in the dish. Season with salt and pepper. Place the bread in the bowl of a food processor and process until fine. Add the garlic, oregano, rosemary, and mustard, and process to mix. With the machine running, slowly add the olive oil through the feed tube and process until smooth. Spread the mixture over the zucchini and bake until the zucchini is tender, about 30 minutes. Serve warm.

SESAME-CHEDDAR CRACKERS

These simple little crackers are actually just another form of shortbread. You can vary them by adding chopped fresh herbs, ground toasted nuts, or even curry powder. Almost every time I entertain, these crackers make an appearance in one form or another, whether I serve them just as a nosh with wine or top them with a crab relish for something a bit fancier.

3 cups flour

1 cup unsalted butter, diced

1¹/₂ cups grated Cheddar cheese

2 cloves garlic, minced

2 tablespoons sesame seeds, lightly toasted (page 186)

1 teaspoon minced canned chipotle chile in adobo sauce, or ¹/₂ teaspoon cayenne pepper

1 teaspoon salt

Preheat the oven to 350°. In the bowl of a food processor, combine the flour, butter, cheese, garlic, sesame seeds, chipotle pepper, and salt, and process until a dough forms on top of the blades. Place the dough on a well-floured board and roll it out to ¹/₄ inch thick. With a 1-inch round or square cookie cutter, cut out the crackers and place on a greased baking sheet. Bake until golden brown, 12 to 15 minutes. Let cool 5 minutes on the sheet and then serve warm, or store in an airtight container for up to 2 days.

SHIITAKE SPRING ROLLS

MAKES 1 DOZEN

Spring rolls are classic finger food for a party, and this rendition pairs earthy shiitakes with a wonderful, piquant dipping sauce. If you're going to make these, I suggest you make a double or even triple batch and then freeze the extras. Then you can quickly fry them whenever the mood strikes.

Dipping Sauce

1/4 cup rice vinegar

2 tablespoons sugar

1 clove garlic, chopped

1 teaspoon peeled, chopped fresh ginger

1/2 teaspoon chopped fresh cilantro

Dash of chile paste

Fish sauce

Shiitake Filling

1 tablespoon vegetable oil

2 cloves garlic, chopped

2 teaspoons peeled, chopped fresh ginger

3 cups sliced fresh shiitake mushrooms

1/2 cup mirin wine

1/3 cup hoisin sauce

3 green onions, minced

2 teaspoons chopped fresh cilantro

1 teaspoon chile paste

Soy sauce

1 dozen spring roll wrappers

Vegetable oil, for deep-frying

12 lettuce leaves

To prepare the dipping sauce: Whisk together all of the dipping sauce ingredients in a small bowl, adding the fish sauce to taste. Set aside.

To prepare the filling: Heat the vegetable oil in a large sauté pan over high heat until very hot. Add the garlic and ginger, and sauté for 2 minutes. Add the mushrooms and sauté just until tender, about 5 minutes. Add the mirin and cook until reduced and the mixture is almost dry, about 4 minutes. Transfer to a bowl and let cool for about 10 minutes. Add the hoisin sauce, green onions, cilantro, chile paste, and soy sauce to taste, and mix well.

To prepare the spring rolls: Place a spring roll wrapper on a flat work surface, with a corner pointing toward you. Place a heaping tablespoon of the filling in the center of the wrapper. Fold the corner closest to you over the filling. Fold the side corners over the filling, then roll up to form a small cigar shape. Continue with the remaining filling and wrappers.

Heat about 4 inches of vegetable oil in a wok or large saucepan over high heat until it reaches 350°. Add as many of the spring rolls as will fit in the pan without overcrowding, and cook until golden brown, about 4 minutes. Drain on paper towels. Continue with the remaining spring rolls.

To serve: Arrange the spring rolls and the lettuce leaves on a platter. Each guest can wrap a spring roll in a lettuce leaf before dipping it in the sauce.

MARK'S JUNGLE RICE

I stole this recipe from Mark Dowers, our chef at the Bistro, who often uses this flavorful rice as a side dish at the restaurant. People can have trouble making perfect rice, but by cooking the basmati rice in this pilaf style there's less to worry about. Since it's cooked in the oven, it will be light and fluffy every time.

1 cup basmati rice
2 teaspoons vegetable oil
2 cloves garlic, chopped
2 teaspoons peeled, chopped fresh ginger
1 cup chicken stock (page 187)
$^1/_2$ cup coconut milk
2 teaspoons chopped fresh basil
2 teaspoons chopped fresh cilantro
2 teaspoons chopped fresh mint
Salt
Freshly ground black pepper

Preheat the oven to 350°. Rinse the rice in a sieve under cold running water until the water runs clear; drain. Heat the vegetable oil in a saucepan over high heat until hot. Add the garlic and ginger and sauté for about 2 minutes. Add the rice and sauté until well coated with the oil, about 1 minute. Add the stock, coconut milk, and herbs, and season to taste with salt and pepper. Bring to a boil. Cover the pan with a lid or foil, set it in the oven, and cook for 15 minutes. Stir well, cover, and cook 15 minutes longer, or until tender. Fluff with a fork just before serving, and adjust the seasonings if needed. Serve hot.

CHILLED FIVE-SPICE PRAWNS with CAPER AIOLI

Because of the expense, you probably won't make these prawns for every party. But when that truly special occasion comes along, you can have absolutely everything made and on a serving tray up to 24 hours in advance, ready to garnish and serve when the doorbell rings.

Five-Spice Prawns

**24 prawns (16 to 20 count), peeled with
    tail remaining**
1 tablespoon extra virgin olive oil
3 cloves garlic, minced
1 tablespoon five-spice powder
Salt
Freshly cracked black pepper

Caper Aioli

1 egg yolk
1 clove garlic
1 tablespoon sherry vinegar
1 teaspoon Dijon mustard
1 cup extra virgin olive oil
$1/4$ cup drained capers, coarsely chopped
2 teaspoons grated lemon zest
1 teaspoon lemon juice
Salt
Freshly cracked black pepper

1 tablespoon grated lemon zest, for garnish
1 tablespoon chopped fresh thyme, for garnish

To prepare the prawns: Oil the grill and heat until very hot (to test, you should be able to hold your hand over the grill for no more than 5 seconds).

While the grill is heating, place the prawns in a large bowl. In a small bowl, whisk together the olive oil, garlic, and five-spice powder. Pour the mixture over the prawns and toss well. Season with salt and cracked pepper. Place the prawns on the hot grill and cook until they just turn pink, 3 to 4 minutes. Transfer the prawns to a plate, let cool for about 10 minutes, and then refrigerate until chilled, 30 to 40 minutes.

To prepare the aioli: Place the egg yolk, garlic, vinegar, and mustard in the bowl of a food processor. With the machine running, slowly add the olive oil through the feed tube, processing until very thick and emulsified. Add the capers, the 2 teaspoons lemon zest, and the lemon juice, and process again briefly to mix. Season to taste with salt and cracked pepper. Refrigerate until ready to serve, or up to 1 week.

To serve: Place the aioli in a bowl and arrange the prawns on a large platter. Sprinkle with the lemon zest and thyme. Serve chilled.

NOTE: Children and individuals who are immunosuppressed should not eat uncooked eggs that have not been pasteurized.

GREEN ONION–BUTTERMILK BISCUITS

MAKES 8

These biscuits aren't just for soups and stews. I serve them for all kinds of occasions, and with just about everything! You can make these up to four hours in advance: Roll and cut them out, place them on a baking sheet, and refrigerate until it's time to bake them. Serve them right out of the oven, so the steam will waft out of the piping hot biscuits as your guests split them open. Remember, biscuits take a delicate touch—if you overhandle them they'll be tough, not tender and flaky.

2 cups flour
1 clove garlic, minced
1 bunch green onions, both green and white parts, minced
1 tablespoon baking powder
1 teaspoon salt
1 cup unsalted butter, diced
$^3/_4$ cup buttermilk

Preheat the oven to 350°. Place the flour, garlic, green onions, baking powder, salt, and butter in a bowl. Using your fingertips, mix just until the mixture resembles a coarse meal. Add the buttermilk, and mix with a fork just until the dough comes together. Form the dough into a ball, place on a well-floured board, and roll out into a $^1/_2$-inch-thick circle. With a 2-inch round cutter, cut out the biscuits and place on a greased baking sheet. Bake until golden brown, about 20 minutes. Serve warm.

CREAMY GARLIC SPINACH

SERVES 4

This is nothing like the creamed spinach you had to choke down as a child. In this tasty side dish, the spinach is just barely cooked, so it still has good texture and flavor, plus the bonus of a creamy, flavorful sauce. You can prepare the sauce up to a day in advance and then reheat it and add the spinach at the last minute.

2 cloves garlic, chopped
1 shallot, chopped
$1/2$ cup dry white wine
1 cup heavy whipping cream
1 bunch spinach, rinsed, stems removed, and spun dry
Pinch nutmeg
Salt
Freshly ground black pepper

Combine the garlic, shallot, and wine in a large sauté pan over high heat and reduce until about 2 tablespoons of liquid remain. Add the cream and reduce until about $1/2$ cup remains. Add the spinach to the sauce, and cook just until the spinach wilts. Add the nutmeg and season well with salt and pepper. Serve immediately.

Essentials for a Well-Stocked Bar

A home bar doesn't need to be an elaborate place you create by adding on to your house or by transforming your basement into a social den reminiscent of the 1970s. A cupboard will suffice. Keeping your bar well stocked doesn't take a whole lot of planning and expense, either. With a few small pieces of bar equipment or tools and a basic supply of ingredients, you can concoct any drink in minutes, just like a professional.

To set up and stock your bar, I suggest the following:

- **Muddler (a small wooden implement used to mash fruit, ice, and herbs such as mint)**
- **Cocktail shaker**
- **Cocktail strainer**
- **Long bar spoon**
- **Zester**
- **Ice (remember, ice can pick up odors from the freezer, so replace or replenish it regularly)**
- **Club soda**
- **Tonic water**
- **A selection of sodas: cola, lemon-lime, and ginger ale**
- **A high-quality bottle of each of the following:**
  - **Gin**
  - **Vodka**
  - **Rum (light and dark)**
  - **Bourbon**
  - **Scotch**
  - **Tequila**
  - **Vermouth (sweet and dry)**
  - **Brandy**
  - **Port**
  - **Sherry**

Keep simple syrup, sweet-and-sour mix, and ginger syrup on hand for making a variety of cocktails.

SIMPLE SYRUP

2 cups water
2 cups sugar

In a saucepan over high heat, bring the water and sugar to a boil. Decrease the heat to medium and simmer for 5 minutes. Let cool. Keep refrigerated for up to 2 months.

SWEET-AND-SOUR MIX:

1¼ cups simple syrup
¾ cup freshly squeezed lemon or lime juice

Combine the simple syrup and lemon juice, and mix well. Keep refrigerated for up to 1 week.

GINGER SYRUP:

2 cups water
2 cups sugar
3 (1-inch-long) slices fresh ginger

In a saucepan over high heat, bring the water, sugar, and ginger to a boil. Decrease the heat to medium and simmer for 5 minutes; remove and discard the ginger. Let cool. Keep refrigerated for up to 2 weeks.

SMOKED SALMON PIZZA

SERVES 8

If I am inspired by another smoked seafood, such as trout or mussels, when I am at the market, I'll substitute that for the smoked salmon. When you prepare the dough for this pizza, why not make a double batch and freeze for a head start on an easy appetizer?

Pizza Dough

1 tablespoon (1 package) active dry yeast

Pinch sugar

1^{1}/$_{4}$ cups warm water

2 tablespoons extra virgin olive oil

2 cloves garlic, chopped

3 cups flour

1 teaspoon salt

1 teaspoon freshly ground black pepper

^{1}/$_{4}$ cup extra virgin olive oil

2 heads roasted garlic (page 185)

8 ounces hot-smoked salmon

4 small Yukon Gold potatoes, blanched and thinly
    sliced (page 188)

8 ounces Parmesan cheese, shaved

^{1}/$_{2}$ cup crème fraîche (page 190) or sour cream

2 teaspoons chopped fresh tarragon

To prepare the dough: Mix together the yeast, sugar, and ^{1}/$_{4}$ cup of the warm water in the bowl of a heavy-duty mixer fitted with the paddle attachment. Let sit until creamy and foamy, about 10 minutes. Add the remaining 1 cup of the olive oil, water, and the garlic and mix well. While mixing on slow speed, add the flour, 1 cup at a time, mixing well after each addition. Add the salt and pepper, and mix on slow speed until the dough is smooth and elastic, about 5 minutes. Transfer the dough to a well-floured board and knead to form a smooth ball. Place the dough in a well-greased bowl, cover with a towel, and let rise until doubled in volume, about 1^{1}/$_{2}$ hours.

To prepare the pizza: Preheat the oven to 425°. In a small bowl, whisk together the olive oil and roasted garlic. Set aside. Cut the dough in half. On a well-floured board, stretch the dough out into two 8-inch circles, and place them in two well-greased 10-inch pizza pans. Spread the roasted garlic mixture over the crusts. Gently break up the salmon and distribute it over the crusts. Top with the potato slices. Bake until golden brown, about 20 minutes. Remove the pizzas from the oven and top with the Parmesan cheese, crème fraîche, and tarragon. Serve warm.

SOCCA

Socca is a crêpe-like pancake that hails from the Mediterranean region. Chickpea flour adds a nutty flavor that is more distinctive than all-purpose flour. I like to serve these at room temperature folded into quarters, then drizzled with rouille and garnished with chopped fresh parsley. If I'm serving these for a crowd, I'll arrange the folded socca on a platter and serve the rouille and a variety of other sauces—such as aioli and baba ghanoush—in bowls for dipping.

1 cup chickpea flour

1 clove garlic, minced

Pinch cayenne pepper

1 teaspoon salt

$^1/_2$ teaspoon freshly ground black pepper

$1^1/_4$ cups cold water, plus additional if needed

2 tablespoons extra virgin olive oil

Red Pepper Rouille (page 108), as an accompaniment

To prepare the batter: Combine the flour, garlic, cayenne pepper, and salt in a mixing bowl, and stir well. Add the water and whisk until smooth. Let the batter stand at least 10 minutes to thicken to the consistency of crêpe batter; whisk in a bit more water if the batter is too thick.

To cook: Heat about a teaspoon of the olive oil in an 8-inch nonstick sauté pan over high heat until very hot. Add about $^1/_4$ cup of batter and immediately swirl the pan to spread the batter into a thin pancake. Cook on one side only until the edges are crispy and golden brown, about 1 minute. Repeat with the remaining batter.

To serve: Fold the socca into quarters. Place one on each plate and drizzle with the rouille. Serve immediately.

EGGPLANT and BLUE CHEESE SPREAD

SERVES 6

I started to make this appetizer at home for dinner parties, and people liked it so much that it went on the menu at the Bistro. You can make the spread up to two days in advance, but it's best when eaten at room temperature, so give it 30 minutes out of the refrigerator before serving.

1 large eggplant, diced
2 teaspoons kosher salt
2 tablespoons extra virgin olive oil
1 small onion, julienned
2 cloves garlic, chopped
3 tablespoons balsamic vinegar
4 ounces Maytag Blue cheese or other blue cheese
Salt
Freshly ground black pepper
Toasted baguette slices or crackers,
       as an accompaniment

Toss the eggplant with the kosher salt, and let sit for about 10 minutes. Heat the olive oil in a large sauté pan over high heat until very hot. Add the eggplant and cook without stirring until browned, 3 to 4 minutes. Toss and cook without stirring, 3 to 4 minutes longer. Add the onion and cook until tender, 3 to 4 minutes. Add the garlic and toss well. Remove the mixture from the heat, add the vinegar, and stir well. Let cool for about 15 minutes, or until tepid. Crumble the blue cheese into the eggplant mixture, and mix well. Season to taste with salt and pepper. Serve with toasted baguette slices or crackers.

POBLANO CHILE DIP

You can prepare this chile dip ahead and have it ready and waiting to be broiled at a moment's notice. It also makes a good sauce for flank steak, polenta, and grilled chicken.

1 tablespoon vegetable oil

1 small onion, minced

3 cloves garlic, chopped

3 fresh jalapeños, seeded and minced

2 large poblano chiles, seeded and minced

8 tomatillos, husks removed and rinsed

2 cups chicken stock (page 187) or roasted vegetable
    stock (page 188)

Salt

Freshly ground black pepper

1 cup crumbled feta cheese

$^{1}/_{2}$ cup grated sharp Cheddar cheese

Baked Tortilla Chips (page 18), as an accompaniment

Heat the oil in a large sauté pan over high heat until hot. Add the onion and garlic, and sauté until the onion just starts to brown, about 5 minutes. Add the jalapeños, poblanos, and tomatillos, and sauté for 3 minutes. Add the stock, lower the heat to medium-high, and cook until the peppers are tender and the stock has reduced until the mixture is almost dry, about 25 minutes. Transfer the mixture to a blender and blend until smooth. Season to taste with salt and pepper.

Preheat the broiler. Place the dip in an oven-proof bowl or casserole. Top with the feta and Cheddar, and broil until bubbly and the cheese is melted, about 5 minutes. Serve warm with tortilla chips.

SAUTÉED BABY BOK CHOY with TOASTED SESAME SAUCE

SERVES 8

Baby bok choy may be difficult for you to find in a regular grocery store. If you're not willing to search it out, use julienned napa cabbage instead. The toasted sesame sauce will keep refrigerated for two weeks. Its nutty flavor lends itself well to other vegetables, such as carrots, green beans, and eggplant.

Toasted Sesame Sauce

2 cloves garlic, minced

1 shallot, minced

2 tablespoons rice vinegar

$1/4$ cup mirin wine

3 tablespoons mushroom soy sauce or
    regular soy sauce

1 tablespoon sesame oil

2 tablespoons sesame seeds, toasted (page 186)

Pinch dried red chile flakes

2 teaspoons vegetable oil

8 baby bok choy, halved lengthwise

$1/4$ cup fried shallots (page 185), for garnish

To prepare the sauce: In a bowl, whisk together all the sauce ingredients. Set aside.

To prepare the bok choy: Heat the vegetable oil in a large sauté pan over high heat until smoking hot. Add the bok choy and sauté for 2 minutes. Add the sauce, toss well, and cook just until the bok choy is crisp-tender, about 4 minutes.

To serve: Place the bok choy on a platter and garnish with the fried shallots. Serve hot.

ORANGE-CHILE NOODLES

This versatile dish can be served warm, at room temperature, or cold; it goes very well with grilled fish or chicken; and it travels well, making it great for picnics. Toss in some grilled vegetables and shredded chicken breast for a light meal.

12 ounces dried Chinese egg noodles or spaghetti

$1/2$ cup vegetable oil

3 cloves garlic, minced

1 tablespoon peeled, minced fresh ginger

Grated zest and juice of 1 orange

1 teaspoon frozen orange juice concentrate, thawed

$1/4$ cup soy sauce

$1/3$ cup sweet hot chile sauce

In a stockpot over high heat, bring about 8 cups of water to a boil. Add the noodles and cook until al dente, 7 to 10 minutes. Drain well and place in a large bowl. Set aside.

In a bowl, whisk together the remaining ingredients. Pour the dressing over the noodles and toss well. Let sit at least 10 minutes before serving.

DAD'S BAKED BEANS

Whenever we have big parties at our house, the cry goes out for my dad's baked beans. It's gotten so that our friends expect them—if we're firing up the grill, Dad's beans had better be there!

1 pound dried pinto beans, rinsed

1 cup dried black beans

1 yellow onion, diced

2 cloves garlic, chopped

2 smoked ham hocks

2 tablespoons peeled, chopped fresh ginger

1 canned chipotle chile in adobo sauce, chopped

1 teaspoon dry mustard

1 teaspoon ground cumin

1 cup brown sugar

2/3 cup molasses

1 tablespoon soy sauce

Salt

Freshly ground black pepper

Place the pinto and black beans in a large stockpot and add cold water to cover. Bring to a boil over medium heat and cook until the beans are tender, about 1^1/$_2$ hours. Drain the beans and place them in a large bowl. Add the onion, garlic, ham hocks, ginger, chipotle pepper, dry mustard, cumin, brown sugar, molasses, and soy sauce, and mix well. Season to taste with salt and pepper.

Preheat the oven to 275°. Place the beans in a Dutch oven or roasting pan, cover, and bake for 4 hours, or until thick and flavorful. Serve warm.

JOHN'S FRIED CORN

SERVES 6

When John was growing up, his dad used to make this corn, and it's still one of his favorites. We often make this when we have big barbecues at our house, because it's easier to deal with than corn on the cob.

2 tablespoons unsalted butter
Kernels cut from 6 ears corn (about 6 cups)
Salt
Freshly cracked black pepper

Heat the butter in a large sauté pan over high heat until melted and bubbly. Add the corn and sauté until tender, 3 to 4 minutes. Season to taste with salt and pepper. Serve warm.

CLAMS with HOT-AND-SOUR SAUCE

SERVES 6

This recipe is a longtime standard of the Bistro's appetizer menu, and I'm constantly asked for the recipe. Paired with a salad, the clams make a perfect light lunch.

Hot-And-Sour Sauce

1 tablespoon vegetable oil

1 small onion, minced

3 cloves garlic, minced

1 tablespoon peeled, chopped fresh ginger

$^1/_2$ cup sake or dry white wine

$^1/_2$ cup clam juice or fish stock (page 186)

$^1/_2$ cup soy sauce

1 tablespoon sugar or cane sugar

Grated zest and juice of 1 lime

1 tablespoon rice vinegar

2 teaspoons chile paste

1 tablespoon cornstarch, dissolved in
    3 tablespoons water

4 pounds fresh clams, rinsed

1 tablespoon chopped fresh basil

Heat the vegetable oil in large sauté pan or a wok over high heat until very hot. Add the onion, garlic, and ginger, and sauté for 2 minutes. Add the sake and cook until the liquid has reduced and the mixture is almost dry, 3 to 4 minutes. Add the clam juice, soy sauce, sugar, lime zest and juice, vinegar, and chile paste, and bring to a boil. Slowly whisk in the cornstarch mixture. Add the clams, cover the pan with a lid, and cook just until the clams open, 8 to 10 minutes. Add the basil and toss.

To serve, divide the clams and sauce among 6 pasta bowls. Serve hot.

BREAD SALAD

This traditional Tuscan dish takes advantage of summer tomatoes and fresh basil. With the addition of a bottle of Chianti, a great group of friends, and a warm summer day, you have the makings of an unforgettable lunch.

6 cups diced day-old, good-quality bread

4 vine-ripened tomatoes, cut into large dice

1 small onion, julienned

4 ounces fresh mozzarella, diced

$1/2$ cup chopped fresh basil

1 small head radicchio, rinsed, spun dry, and
     torn into pieces

$2/3$ cup extra virgin olive oil

$1/4$ cup good-quality sherry vinegar

2 cloves garlic, minced

Salt

Freshly cracked black pepper

Place the bread in a large bowl. Add the tomatoes, onion, mozzarella, basil, and radicchio, and toss well. In a small bowl, whisk together the olive oil, vinegar, and garlic. Pour the dressing over the salad and toss well. Let sit at room temperature for at least 30 minutes or up to 2 hours, then season to taste with salt and pepper. Serve at room temperature.

Cheese

When I entertain, cheese always makes an appearance, whether as an appetizer enjoyed with glasses of crisp Pinot Gris or as a separate course served after dessert. Years ago, the selection of cheese found in the average grocery store was limited. Today, thankfully, we can buy a full spectrum of cheese from countries around the world—and even the smallest of stores offers a better choice than what the large stores offered ten years ago. The introduction of such a wonderful palette of cheese to our taste buds has inspired a rebirth in American artisan cheese making. This means I can serve a beautiful aged Gouda from Holland alongside a fresh goat cheese made just miles away on a Willamette Valley farm.

If I serve cheese as a starter with wine or cocktails, I always like to offer one mild slicing cheese, such as Emmentaler; a soft cheese, such as Montrachet or a local goat cheese; and a more pungent cheese to round things out, such as Maytag Blue or Stilton. To complement the variety of textures and flavors in the cheese, I like to serve a combination of crackers, crostini, and breads.

To serve cheese as a separate course before dessert or even as dessert itself, I take some of the same principles into consideration as I do when serving it as an appetizer. For example, I'll serve a slicing cheese like Black Diamond Cheddar; a soft, ripe Camembert; and something a bit stronger, such as Parmigiano-Reggiano. To this I'll add fruit, such as grapes or sliced pears and apples. If dessert will follow, be sure to keep in mind how rich cheese can be; usually just a taste of each is enough to please the palate while still letting your guests look forward to an enticing dessert. If you are concluding the meal with cheese instead of dessert, put the selections on a tray so your guests can determine just how much they want. Either way, remember that you want your guests to feel satisfied, not overwhelmed.

ROASTED BABY NEW POTATOES with OLIVE TAPENADE

SERVES 8

Make this easy snack when you want to serve passed appetizers or quick bites.

Olive Tapenade
$1/4$ **cup cured black olives, pitted**
$1/4$ **cup cured green olives, pitted**
2 cloves garlic
$1/2$ **teaspoon drained capers**
1 anchovy fillet
1 teaspoon lemon juice
2 tablespoons extra virgin olive oil

12 small (about the size of a golf ball) new potatoes, rinsed and halved
1 tablespoon extra virgin olive oil
Salt
Freshly ground black pepper
$1/4$ **cup crème fraîche (page 190)**

To prepare the tapenade: In the bowl of a food processor, combine the olives, garlic, capers, anchovy, and lemon juice, and process until the olives are finely chopped. With the motor running, slowly add the olive oil and process just until mixed. Set aside.

To prepare the potatoes: Preheat the oven to 425°. Using a melon baller, scoop out the center of each potato. Pour the olive oil into a heavy roasting pan, and heat it in the oven until smoking hot. Season the potatoes with salt and pepper, then place them cut side down in the oil, and roast until tender, 15 to 20 minutes. Let cool to room temperature. Fill the potatoes with a heaping teaspoonful of the tapenade, then top with a small dollop of crème fraîche.

Illustrated on page 22b

STEAMED CAULIFLOWER with SUNDRIED TOMATOES and ROASTED GARLIC

SERVES 6

I know cauliflower is not everyone's favorite vegetable, but when topped with sundried tomatoes and roasted garlic, this much-maligned vegetable may become the hit of the dinner party.

2 tablespoons minced dry-packed sundried tomatoes

1 head roasted garlic (page 185)

1 clove garlic, chopped

1 tablespoon sherry vinegar

1 teaspoon chopped fresh oregano

3 tablespoons extra virgin olive oil

Salt

Freshly ground black pepper

1 large head cauliflower, cut into florets

$^1/_2$ cup toasted bread crumbs (page 185)

To prepare the sauce: In a small bowl, stir together the sundried tomatoes, roasted garlic, garlic, vinegar, oregano, and olive oil until well mixed. Season to taste with salt and pepper, and set aside.

To prepare the cauliflower: In a large pot of boiling salted water, cook the cauliflower until crisp-tender, about 4 minutes. Drain well.

To serve: Place the cauliflower on a platter, top with the breadcrumbs, and drizzle with the sauce. Serve hot.

The BEST MASHED POTATOES

SERVES 6

When we teach our Thanksgiving class at the Bistro cooking school, our students are often surprised when we suggest preparing mashed potatoes a few hours in advance and reheating them in a double boiler before serving. The classical method of preparing mashed potatoes by ricing instead of mashing gives these potatoes a lighter texture. Drying the diced, boiled potatoes in the oven before ricing means I can add even more cream and butter—and, of course, that's another reason why they are simply the best! For variations, mix in roasted garlic, diced roasted poblano chiles, blue cheese, fresh herbs, wasabi powder, or curry powder.

2 pounds Yukon Gold potatoes, peeled and diced
4 whole cloves garlic, peeled
$1/2$ cup heavy whipping cream
2 tablespoons unsalted butter
Salt
Freshly ground black pepper

Preheat the oven to 350°. Place the potatoes and garlic in a large saucepan and add enough water to cover. Cover and cook over medium heat until very tender, about 10 minutes. Drain well. Arrange the potatoes and garlic in a single layer on a baking sheet. Bake for about 10 minutes to dry the potatoes, taking care not to let a crust form. Transfer the potatoes to a ricer, and rice them into a large bowl. Set aside.

Heat the cream and butter in a small saucepan over high heat just until the cream comes to a boil. Pour the mixture over the potatoes, and mix well. Season to taste with salt and pepper, and mix well. Serve warm. (The potatoes can be made up to 2 hours in advance. Place them in a metal bowl, cover with plastic wrap or foil, and set the bowl over a simmering water bath until ready to serve.)

FRENCH FRIES

SERVES 6

I know, with all the slicing and deep-frying, French fries are not the easiest side dish to pre-pare for a dinner party. On the other hand, if you're having a few friends over for a casual dinner, it can be a great time to make them. My technique for preparing French fries has a few more steps, but it yields super-crispy fries—the best you'll ever taste!

Vegetable oil, for deep-frying
**6 large Yukon Gold potatoes, julienned, placed in
      a bowl, and covered with cold water**
Salt
Freshly ground black pepper

Heat 6 inches of oil in a large, heavy saucepan over high heat until it reaches 350°. Drain the potatoes well, add as many as will fit in the pan of hot oil without overcrowding, and blanch 2 to 3 minutes. Drain the fries on paper towels, transfer them to a baking sheet, and place in the freezer until chilled (but not frozen). Continue with the remaining potatoes.

Let the oil heat back up to 350°. Again work-ing in batches, add the blanched fries, and fry until golden brown, about 4 minutes. Drain on paper towels. Season to taste with salt and pepper. Serve warm.

OVEN HOME FRIES

SERVES 8

These fries are similar to something you would see at breakfast, but I like to pair them with grilled steaks or pork chops. They are finished in the oven, which leaves you free to pull together any last-minute details of the rest of the dinner.

2 tablespoons extra virgin olive oil
1 medium onion, diced
2 red bell peppers, seeded and diced
6 large Yukon Gold potatoes, peeled and diced
3 cloves garlic, minced
Salt
Freshly ground black pepper

Preheat the oven to 425°. Heat the olive oil in a very large ovenproof sauté pan over high heat until smoking hot. Add the onion and sauté until lightly browned, about 4 minutes. Add the peppers and sauté until tender, about 4 minutes. Add the potatoes and let them brown, without stirring, on one side, 3 to 4 minutes. Toss well. Place the pan on the bottom rack of the oven, and bake the potatoes until tender, about 15 minutes. Remove the pan from the oven, stir in the garlic, and season well with salt and pepper. Serve hot.

MARINATED SWEET PEPPERS

SERVES 6

Prepare this in the summer when peppers are abundant. You can serve the peppers as a simple appetizer with crostini to ease into a summer gathering, or even as an addition to an antipasto plate.

6 red, yellow, or orange bell peppers, roasted, peeled, and seeded (page 186)

2 tablespoons balsamic vinegar

3 tablespoons extra virgin olive oil

1 clove garlic, chopped

6 basil leaves, julienned

Kosher salt

Freshly cracked black pepper

2 ounces arugula, rinsed and spun dry, for garnish

Cut the peppers into $1/2$-inch-wide strips and place on a large plate or platter. In a small bowl, whisk together the vinegar, olive oil, and garlic. Drizzle the marinade over the peppers. Sprinkle with the basil and season well with salt and pepper. Let stand at least 30 minutes before serving. Garnish with arugula.

MARINATED OLIVES

SERVES 6

These olives are great to nibble on before dinner with a glass of wine or even between courses. Since they hold up so well, you can make a double batch and serve them at a moment's notice, either for a snack or for a dinner party.

2 cups mixed cured olives, drained

1¹/₂ cups extra virgin olive oil, plus additional if needed

3 cloves garlic, peeled

Zest of 1 lemon

3 sprigs rosemary, cut into 3-inch pieces

¹/₂ teaspoon dried red chile flakes

¹/₂ teaspoon freshly cracked black pepper

Place the olives in a small crock or bowl. Pour enough olive oil over the olives to just cover. Add the garlic, lemon zest, rosemary, chile flakes, and pepper, and mix well. Cover and refrigerate at least 24 hours, or up to 1 month. Let stand at room temperature for at least 30 minutes before serving.

DEEP-FRIED PRAWNS with THREE-ONION CHUTNEY

SERVES 6

This Indian-inspired appetizer has been on the Bistro's menu for quite some time. When you cook this in your home, do what we do at the restaurant: clean the prawns, make the chutney, and prepare the batter in advance. That way, all you'll need to do is dip and fry the prawns right before serving.

Three-Onion Chutney

2 tablespoons olive oil

4 large shallots, peeled and cut into eighths

1 large yellow onion, julienned

1 large red onion, julienned

3 cloves garlic, chopped

1 tablespoon peeled, chopped fresh ginger

$^1/_2$ cup dry sherry

$^1/_4$ cup brown sugar

$^1/_4$ cup rice vinegar

2 teaspoons curry powder, toasted (page 186)

1 teaspoon chile paste, or to taste

Pinch ground cumin

Salt

Freshly ground black pepper

Batter

$1^1/_2$ cups chickpea flour

3 cloves garlic, minced

2 teaspoons ground cumin

1 teaspoon cayenne pepper

Pinch ground turmeric

$^1/_2$ teaspoon baking soda

$1^1/_2$ to 2 cups water

About 2 quarts vegetable oil, for deep-frying

20 prawns (16 to 20 count), peeled and deveined

Salt

Freshly ground black pepper

$^1/_2$ cup plain yogurt, as an accompaniment

To prepare the chutney: Heat the olive oil in a large sauté pan over high heat until hot. Add the shallots and onions and cook without stirring until they start to brown, 3 to 5 minutes. Toss and cook again without stirring until brown, 3 to 5 minutes. Toss and continue cooking until well caramelized, about 15 to 20 minutes total cooking time. Add the garlic and ginger and sauté for 2 minutes. Add the sherry and sugar and cook until the sherry has reduced and the mixture is almost dry, 3 to 4 minutes. Add the vinegar and curry powder and cook about 2 minutes. Add the chile paste and cumin, and season to taste with salt and pepper. Stir well. Set aside.

To prepare the batter: Whisk together the chickpea flour, garlic, cumin, cayenne pepper, turmeric, and baking soda in a mixing bowl. Add the water and whisk until smooth (whisk in additional water if the batter is too thick).

To deep-fry the prawns: Heat 6 inches of vegetable oil in a large saucepan over high heat until it reaches 350° (or when a small piece of bread browns in the oil in about 30 seconds). Season the prawns with salt and pepper. Dip the prawns in the batter, and place as many as will fit in the oil without overcrowding. Cook until golden brown, about 4 minutes. Drain on paper towels. Repeat with the remaining prawns.

To serve: Place the prawns on a serving platter and serve with the chutney and yogurt.

salads and
soups

Grilled Vegetable Salad with Smoked
    Mozzarella / 52

Olive-Dressed Greens / 53

Corn and Chile Bisque / 54

Oyster Stew / 55

White Bean and Prosciutto Soup / 56

Oven-Roasted Goat Cheese Salad with
    Arugula / 57

Curried Carrot Soup / 60

Green Bean and Mint Salad / 61

Red Mussel Chowder / 62

Spinach Salad with Pear-Thyme
    Vinaigrette / 63

Cappy's Old-Fashioned Chicken Noodle
    Soup / 64

Roasted Potato and Fennel Salad / 65

Portobello Mushroom Soup / 66

Fennel and Celeriac Salad with Mustard Seed
    Dressing / 67

GRILLED VEGETABLE SALAD with SMOKED MOZZARELLA

SERVES 8

This is one of the dishes John and I serve when we teach our grilling and barbecue classes. Even though our students get to try everything from ribs to smoked salmon, this salad is always one of their favorites. When I prepare this at home for a dinner party, I grill the vegetables and toss the salad before anyone arrives. Since the salad is better at room temperature, I just cover it and let it sit until I'm ready to serve it. That way, I have one less thing to worry about— plus I don't overload the barbecue if the main course is also grilled.

Marinade

¹/₄ cup balsamic vinegar

3 cloves garlic, chopped

2 tablespoons chopped fresh basil

1 tablespoon freshly cracked black pepper

³/₄ cup extra virgin olive oil

1 eggplant, cut crosswise into ¹/₂-inch-thick slices

4 large portobello mushrooms

1 large sweet onion, cut crosswise into ¹/₂-inch-thick slices

2 zucchini, cut lengthwise into ¹/₂-inch-thick slices

2 yellow squash, cut lengthwise into ¹/₂-inch-thick slices

1 red bell pepper, roasted, peeled, seeded, and julienned (page 186)

4 ounces smoked mozzarella, cut into small dice

Salt

Basil sprigs, for garnish

To marinate the vegetables: In a large bowl, whisk together the vinegar, garlic, basil, pepper, and olive oil. Place the vegetables in the marinade and toss gently. Marinate at room temperature for at least 30 minutes, or refrigerate for up to 2 hours.

To grill the vegetables and assemble the salad: Oil the grill and heat until very hot (to test, you should be able to hold your hand over the grill for no more than 5 seconds). Remove the vegetables from the marinade and drain well, reserving the marinade. Place the vegetables on the grill and grill until crisp-tender, 4 to 8 minutes, depending on the vegetable. Chop coarsely and place in a large bowl. Add about ¹/₂ cup of the reserved marinade, or enough to coat the vegetables. Add the smoked mozzarella and mix well. Season to taste with salt and mix well. Serve warm, at room temperature, or chilled, garnished with basil sprigs.

OLIVE-DRESSED GREENS

SERVES 6

Everyone needs a good salad dressing recipe as an alternative to run-of-the-mill oil and vinegar or ranch. I created the dressing for this salad using good-quality cured green olives, which lend texture and tang—making it anything but common.

Green Olive Dressing
2 tablespoons sherry vinegar
1 shallot, chopped
2 cloves garlic, chopped
1 teaspoon Dijon mustard
$1/_3$ cup chopped cured green olives
2 anchovy fillets, mashed
$1/_3$ cup extra virgin olive oil
Salt
Freshly cracked black pepper

1 head red leaf lettuce, rinsed, spun dry, and gently
    torn into smaller pieces
4 ounces mesclun mix, rinsed and spun dry
2 vine-ripened tomatoes, quartered
1 cucumber, thinly sliced
6 thin slices red onion

To prepare the dressing: In a small bowl, whisk together the vinegar, shallot, garlic, mustard, green olives, and anchovies. While whisking, slowly add the olive oil and whisk until thick and emulsified. Season to taste with salt and pepper. Set aside. (The dressing can be prepared in advance and kept refrigerated for up to 2 weeks).

To assemble the salad: Place the greens in a large bowl. Add the dressing and toss well. Arrange the tomatoes, cucumber, and red onion on top. Serve immediately.

CORN and CHILE BISQUE

SERVES 8

This is one of my favorite soups to serve when I entertain in late summer, and on really hot days, I'll serve it chilled. The velvety texture of the bisque contrasts nicely with the spike of the chiles, showcasing corn at the peak of its season. If other seasonal ingredients at the market that day inspire me—such as opal basil, heirloom tomatoes, or even a piquant cayenne pepper—I'll add them to the soup to vary the texture and flavor.

1 tablespoon extra virgin olive oil

1 onion, minced

3 cloves garlic, chopped

1 cup dry sherry

Kernels cut from 4 ears corn (about 4 cups)

2 Yukon Gold potatoes, peeled and diced

4 poblano chiles, roasted, peeled, seeded, and diced
(page 186)

2 red bell peppers, roasted, peeled, seeded, and diced
(page 186)

4 cups vegetable stock (page 188)

2 cups heavy whipping cream

Juice of $1/2$ lime

2 teaspoons ground cumin, toasted (page 186)

1 teaspoon chopped fresh cilantro

Salt

Freshly ground black pepper

$1/2$ cup sour cream

Cilantro sprigs, for garnish

Heat the olive oil in a stockpot over high heat until very hot. Add the onion and garlic, and sauté for 2 minutes. Add the sherry and reduce over high heat until about $1/4$ cup of liquid remains. Add the corn, potatoes, chiles, peppers, and stock, and simmer until the potatoes are tender, about 10 minutes. Transfer the soup to a blender and purée (or purée with a handheld blender). Return the soup to the pot, add the cream, and reduce over high heat for about 15 minutes. Add the lime juice, cumin, and cilantro, mix well, and season to taste with salt and pepper. Serve in individual bowls, topped with a dollop of sour cream and garnished with a cilantro sprig.

OYSTER STEW

Oyster stew is very simple, yet quite elegant. Ideally, use the freshest oysters that are in season, and shuck them yourself (I like Kumamotos or Hama Hamas). If you buy them preshucked, be sure to get the extra-small size. You can prepare the stew base in advance and keep it refrigerated for up to three days, or frozen for up to six months. To reheat without separating, first bring about $^1/_2$ cup of heavy cream to a boil. Slowly whisk in the cold base, and bring it to a boil. It should be smooth and emulsified.

Oyster Stew Base

3 cloves garlic, chopped

2 shallots, chopped

1 cup dry white wine

1 cup dry sherry

6 cups fish stock (page 186)

3 cups heavy whipping cream

1 teaspoon vegetable oil

2 teaspoons peeled, chopped fresh ginger

2 cloves garlic, chopped

20 freshly shucked oysters

1 red bell pepper, julienned

2 teaspoons chopped fresh thyme

2 teaspoons chopped fresh flat-leaf parsley

Salt

Freshly ground black pepper

1 tablespoon unsalted butter

To prepare the stew base: In a large stockpot over high heat, combine the garlic, shallots, wine, and sherry. Bring the mixture to a boil and reduce until about $^1/_2$ cup of liquid remains, 5 to 6 minutes. Add the fish stock and reduce until about 2 cups of liquid remain, about 15 minutes. Add the cream and reduce until about 4 cups of liquid remain, about 15 minutes. Keep warm until ready to serve, or let cool, transfer to another container, and refrigerate.

To finish the stew: Heat the oil in a very large sauté pan over high heat until very hot. Add the ginger and garlic and sauté for 1 minute. Add the oysters, peppers, herbs, and stew base and bring just to a boil. Season to taste with salt and pepper.

To serve: Ladle the stew into large, shallow bowls, and top each with about $^1/_2$ teaspoon of butter. Serve immediately.

WHITE BEAN and PROSCIUTTO SOUP

SERVES 8

White beans are so satisfying that with a salad, this soup could easily become a meal. For a casual gathering, make the soup a day in advance. When your friends arrive, all you'll need to do is reheat the soup and serve.

1½ cups dried cannellini beans or other white beans, sorted and rinsed

1 tablespoon extra virgin olive oil

3 cloves garlic, chopped

1 onion, minced

1 cup dry sherry

5 cups chicken stock (page 187)

2 teaspoons chopped fresh rosemary

2 teaspoons chopped fresh oregano

2 teaspoons chopped fresh thyme

2 red bell peppers, roasted, peeled, seeded, and diced (page 186)

4 ounces prosciutto, julienned

Salt

Freshly ground black pepper

⅓ cup freshly grated Parmesan cheese

Place the beans in a large bowl. Cover with cold water and let them soak at least 24 hours. Drain.

Heat the olive oil in a large stockpot over high heat until very hot. Add the garlic and onion and sauté about 2 minutes. Add the sherry and cook until reduced by about one-half. Add the beans and chicken stock, and cook just until the beans are al dente, about 20 minutes. Add the rosemary, oregano, and thyme, and cook until the beans are very tender, about 15 minutes. Stir in the peppers and prosciutto, and season to taste with salt and pepper. Serve in individual bowls, topped with a bit of Parmesan cheese.

OVEN-ROASTED GOAT CHEESE SALAD with ARUGULA

SERVES 6

Since this salad is so substantial, it can also be served as an appetizer. To make serving a breeze, make the dressing up to two weeks in advance, and prepare the goat cheese rounds up to a day ahead. Clean the arugula up to three hours before serving, place it in a large bowl, cover with a damp paper towel and then plastic wrap, and refrigerate. All you'll need to do before serving is warm the goat cheese and toss the greens with the dressing.

Whole-Grain Mustard Vinaigrette

1 clove garlic, chopped

1 shallot, chopped

2 tablespoon sherry vinegar

1 teaspoon Dijon mustard

2 teaspoons whole-grain mustard

1/2 cup extra virgin olive oil

Salt

Freshly ground black pepper

8 ounces soft mild goat cheese

1 cup bread crumbs, toasted (page 185)

1/2 teaspoon cracked black pepper

1 teaspoon chopped fresh basil

1 teaspoon chopped fresh thyme

1 teaspoon chopped fresh rosemary

2 teaspoons extra virgin olive oil

8 ounces arugula, rinsed and spun dry

To prepare the dressing: In a bowl, whisk together the garlic, shallot, vinegar, and mustards. While whisking, slowly add the olive oil and whisk until thick and emulsified. Season to taste with salt and pepper, and mix well. Set aside until ready to serve.

To prepare the goat cheese: Preheat the oven to 350°. Divide the cheese into 6 pieces, and form each piece into a patty. In a small bowl, combine the bread crumbs, pepper, basil, thyme, and rosemary, and mix well; transfer to a plate. Dredge the cheese well in the bread crumb mixture. Heat the olive oil in an oven-proof sauté pan over high heat until very hot. Add the cheese and cook on just one side until brown, about 3 minutes. Flip the cheese, set the pan in the oven, and bake until warm, 3 to 4 minutes.

To assemble and serve the salad: While the goat cheese is baking, in a large bowl, toss the arugula with the dressing. Distribute the arugula among 6 salad plates. Top each salad with a piece of warm goat cheese. Serve immediately.

Entertaining off the Cuff:

TIPS FOR STOCKING YOUR PANTRY FOR LAST-MINUTE ENTERTAINING

Some of the best parties are those that happen unexpectedly: A conversation over the fence with your neighbors leads to an impromptu barbecue out on the deck, a day spent shopping with friends extends into evening, or your favorite cousin calls on his way through town—just before dinner time. Having a well-stocked pantry is the key to looking like the experienced, unflappable host who can pull together a meal at a moment's notice.

Here are twenty items I like to keep on hand, so no matter when a gathering is suddenly in the works, I can simply welcome our friends, open the wine, rummage through the pantry for inspiration, and whip up dinner:

• Dried pasta.

• A jar of good-quality tomato sauce. Just add some goat cheese and fresh herbs for a simple, delicious pasta dish.

• Good-quality extra virgin olive oil. It's indispensable for everything from sautéing to drizzling over bruschetta.

• Frozen homemade or canned chicken stock.

• Fresh onions and garlic, the basis of all savory cooking.

• A variety of cured olives. Snack on them or use them to make tapenade.

• Mustard. Dijon or other gourmet mustards can add zip to a sauce, dressing, or soup.

• Bittersweet chocolate. Use it to make a quick flourless torte or chocolate sauce for ice cream, or grate it over fresh berries.

• Soy sauce.

• Sweet hot chile sauce. Use it as a dipping sauce or to baste grilled fish, meat, or chicken.

- A bottle or two of both red and white wine. It doesn't have to be expensive, just quaffable.

- Fresh eggs. A delicious omelet or frittata makes a satisfying entrée anytime.

- Good-quality aged Parmesan cheese.

- Balsamic vinegar that has been aged for at least five years. Use it to finish sauces and in last-minute dressings.

- Arborio rice, the key ingredient in risotto.

- A frozen loaf of good-quality bread. Quickly defrost it and serve it to round out any meal.

- Fresh and dried herbs.

- A selection of good-quality spices, such as cumin, coriander, curry powder, peppercorns, cayenne pepper, chile powder, and cinnamon. Store spices in a cool, dry cupboard and keep for no longer than one year.

- Wines for cooking, such as dry sherry and mirin.

- Fresh ginger. You can keep it in the freezer, or place it in a small jar, add dry sherry to cover, and refrigerate for up to 2 weeks.

CURRIED CARROT SOUP

SERVES 8

Toasting the spices in the hot oil intensifies them and infuses the carrots with an incredible flavor. This soup is a great way to open a meal, but stir in grilled shrimp or chicken and it could also stand alone as an entrée.

2 teaspoons ground cumin

1 teaspoon ground coriander

1 tablespoon peeled, chopped fresh ginger

1 teaspoon chile powder

1 teaspoon paprika

$1/2$ teaspoon ground turmeric

$1/4$ teaspoon ground cinnamon

3 cloves garlic, chopped

1 tablespoon vegetable oil

1 yellow onion, minced

1 cup mirin wine

8 small carrots, peeled and diced

1 large celeriac, peeled and diced

1 (12-ounce) can coconut milk

4 cups roasted vegetable stock (page 188)

$1/2$ cup heavy whipping cream

Soy sauce

$1/3$ cup plain yogurt

Combine the cumin, coriander, ginger, chile powder, paprika, turmeric, cinnamon, and garlic in a small bowl and mix well. Heat the oil in a large stockpot over high heat until very hot. Add the spice mixture and toast, stirring often, until fragrant, about 2 minutes. Add the onion and sauté for 1 minute. Add the mirin and cook until the liquid has reduced and the mixture is almost dry, 6 to 8 minutes. Add the carrots, celeriac, coconut milk, and stock, and cook until the carrots are very tender, 15 to 20 minutes. Transfer the mixture to a blender and purée, and then return it to the stockpot. Add the cream, mix well, and bring to a simmer. Season to taste with soy sauce. Serve hot, topped with a dollop of yogurt.

GREEN BEAN and MINT SALAD

SERVES 8

My favorite time to make this salad is early summer, when green beans are super fresh and tender. I especially like to use haricots verts, which are small French green beans that are incredibly sweet. I serve this salad when John and I have small get-togethers around the barbecue; it's also good for picnics.

2¹/₂ pounds fresh green beans, blanched and shocked (page 188)

1 red onion, julienned

2 cloves garlic, chopped

2 tablespoons chopped fresh mint

Grated zest and juice of 1 lemon

2 teaspoons Dijon mustard

¹/₄ cup extra virgin olive oil

¹/₂ cup sour cream

6 dashes Tabasco sauce

Salt

Freshly ground black pepper

Place the green beans and red onion in a large bowl. In a small bowl, whisk together the garlic, mint, lemon zest and juice, and mustard. While whisking, slowly add the olive oil and whisk until thick and emulsified. Whisk in the sour cream and Tabasco. Season to taste with salt and pepper. Pour the dressing over the beans and toss well. Refrigerate at least 30 minutes or up to 24 hours before serving.

RED MUSSEL CHOWDER

SERVES 6

If you decide to prepare this chowder ahead of time, I suggest that you leave the mussels out until just before serving—otherwise, the mussels become overcooked and resemble little rubber bands.

2 pounds fresh mussels, rinsed and debearded

$1/3$ cup dry white wine

1 tablespoon unsalted butter

2 teaspoons extra virgin olive oil

8 slices pepper bacon, diced

1 onion, diced

3 cloves garlic, chopped

1 cup dry red wine

2 cups fish stock (page 186)

4 cups tomato purée

3 Yukon Gold potatoes, peeled and diced

1 tablespoon chopped fresh oregano

1 teaspoon chopped fresh thyme

1 teaspoon chopped fresh marjoram

Salt

Freshly ground black pepper

$1/2$ cup crème fraîche (page 190)

In a large saucepan over high heat, combine the mussels, white wine, and butter. Bring the mixture to a boil and cook just until the mussels open, 6 to 8 minutes. Remove the mussels from the cooking liquid and let cool. Strain the cooking liquid through a fine sieve and set aside. When the mussels are cool enough to handle, remove the meat from the shells and set aside, discarding the shells.

Heat the olive oil in a stockpot over high heat until hot. Add the bacon and cook until crispy, about 4 minutes. Remove the bacon from the pan (reserving the drippings in the pan) drain on paper towels, and set aside. Add the onion and garlic to the pan, lower the heat to medium, and sauté for 2 minutes. Add the red wine and reduce over high heat until about $1/2$ cup of wine remains, about 4 minutes. Add the stock and mussel cooking liquid and reduce until about 1 cup of liquid remains. Add the tomato purée, potatoes, oregano, thyme, and marjoram, and cook until the potatoes are tender, about 10 minutes. Season to taste with salt and pepper. Stir in the mussels and bacon. Serve in individual bowls, topped with a dollop of crème fraîche.

SPINACH SALAD with PEAR-THYME VINAIGRETTE

SERVES 4

Have everything for this flavorful salad ready in advance, so you can quickly toss it together right before serving. The dressing will keep, re-frigerated, for up to a week. Clean the greens up to three hours ahead, place them in a large bowl, cover with a damp paper towel and then plastic wrap, and refrigerate.

Pear-Thyme Vinaigrette

1 pear, peeled, seeded, and diced

$1/4$ cup dry white wine

$1/4$ cup rice vinegar

1 shallot, minced

2 cloves garlic, chopped

2 teaspoons Dijon mustard

$3/4$ cup extra virgin olive oil

2 teaspoons chopped fresh thyme

Salt

Freshly cracked black pepper

1 bunch spinach, rinsed, spun dry, and torn into
    smaller pieces

1 small head radicchio, rinsed, spun dry, and torn into
    smaller pieces

1 cup sliced mushrooms

1 pear, cored and sliced

To prepare the dressing: Combine the pear and wine in a small sauté pan over high heat and cook, stirring often, until the pears are very tender, about 4 minutes. Transfer the pear mixture to a food processor or blender, and add the vinegar, shallot, garlic, and mustard. With the machine running, slowly add the olive oil and process until smooth. Add the thyme and season to taste with salt and pepper. Process again briefly to mix. Refrigerate until ready to use.

To assemble the salad: Place the greens in a large bowl. Add the mushrooms, sliced pears, and about $3/4$ cup of the dressing, and toss well. Serve immediately.

CAPPY'S OLD-FASHIONED CHICKEN NOODLE SOUP

SERVES 6

When John and I have just a couple of friends over to watch a movie, the evening calls for a cozy dish—and it just doesn't get any cozier than this chicken noodle soup!

1 roasting chicken, cut into pieces

6 cups chicken stock (page 187)

1 tablespoon extra virgin olive oil

3 cloves garlic, chopped

1 onion, diced

3 ribs celery, diced

3 medium carrots, peeled and diced

1 cup Madeira or dry sherry

2 bay leaves

3 red bell peppers, roasted, peeled, seeded, and diced
    (page 186)

1 tablespoon chopped fresh basil

2 teaspoons chopped fresh thyme

2 teaspoons chopped fresh rosemary

8 ounces dried egg noodles, cooked al dente

2 tablespoons cayenne sauce

Salt

Freshly ground black pepper

Place the chicken in a large saucepan, cover with the stock, and bring to a simmer over medium heat. Simmer the chicken until just cooked through, about 15 minutes. Remove the chicken from the stock and set aside. Skim and discard the fat from the surface of the stock and discard. Heat the olive oil in a large stockpot over high heat until very hot. Add the garlic, onion, celery, and carrots, and sauté briefly, about 3 minutes. Add the Madeira and cook until it is reduced by one-half. Add the reserved chicken stock and the bay leaves and reduce over medium heat for about 10 minutes. Stir in the peppers, basil, thyme, and rosemary, and cook 10 minutes longer.

Meanwhile, pull the chicken meat off of the bones. Add the chicken, noodles, and cayenne sauce to the soup and cook just until the chicken is heated through. Season to taste with salt and pepper. Serve the soup warm with additional cayenne sauce on the side.

ROASTED POTATO and FENNEL SALAD

SERVES 8

Since this potato salad can be served warm or cold, you can be ahead of the game and prepare it up to a day or two ahead of time. Or, if you run short on time, prepare it at the last minute and serve it warm or at room temperature.

2 tablespoons extra virgin olive oil

14 small Yukon Gold potatoes (about 3 pounds), quartered

3 bulbs fennel, cut into large dice

3 cloves garlic, chopped

2 shallots, minced

1 tablespoon Dijon mustard

¹/₄ cup white wine vinegar

1 cup extra virgin olive oil

2 tablespoons chopped fresh fennel greens

2 teaspoons chopped fresh tarragon

2 tablespoons capers

Salt

Freshly ground black pepper

To prepare the fennel and potatoes: Preheat the oven to 375°. Place the oil in a roasting pan and heat it in the oven until smoking hot. Add the potatoes and roast for about 10 minutes. Add the fennel and roast until the potatoes are tender, about 10 minutes longer. Place the potato mixture in a large bowl. Let cool about 5 minutes.

To prepare the dressing: In a small bowl, whisk together the garlic, shallots, mustard, and vinegar. While whisking, slowly add the olive oil and whisk until thick and emulsified. Add the fennel greens, tarragon, and capers, and mix well. Season to taste with salt and pepper.

To assemble the salad: Pour the dressing over the potatoes and fennel, and toss well. Adjust the seasonings if needed. Serve the salad warm, at room temperature, or cold.

PORTOBELLO MUSHROOM SOUP

Portobellos have a meaty texture and a rich flavor, making this easy-to-prepare soup very hearty. For a more exotic flavor, try substituting seasonal wild mushrooms, such as morels or chanterelles. When you entertain with soup, there's so little to worry about. Soup is usually better the next day, so if you make it in advance all you have to do is set the table, reheat the soup, and open the wine.

8 thin slices (about $\frac{1}{3}$ pound) pancetta or
    pepper bacon

2 teaspoons extra virgin olive oil

1 small onion, diced

3 cloves garlic, chopped

1 cup red wine

5 large portobello mushrooms, diced (discard stems)

3 medium Yukon Gold potatoes, peeled and diced

4 cups chicken stock (page 187)

1 tablespoon chopped fresh thyme

Salt

Freshly cracked black pepper

In a large stockpot over high heat, cook the pancetta until very crispy. Drain well on paper towels and set aside. Add the olive oil to the pot and heat until very hot. Add the onion and garlic and sauté about 2 minutes. Add the red wine and scrape the bottom of the pan to deglaze. Cook until the wine is reduced by about one-half, about 5 minutes. Add the mushrooms, potatoes, stock, and thyme, and simmer until the potatoes are tender, about 10 minutes. Season to taste with salt and lots of cracked black pepper. Stir in the pancetta just before serving.

FENNEL and CELERIAC SALAD with MUSTARD SEED DRESSING

SERVES 6

Celeriac is probably the ugliest root on earth, but under its thick, brown, knobby outer layer lies a delicately flavored, crisp vegetable. When paired with the licorice flavor of fennel and the mustard-infused dressing, it makes a versatile side dish. It's delicious served year-round, either for a barbecue or with something as elegant as seared halibut.

Mustard Seed Dressing

$1/2$ cup dry white wine

1 tablespoon mustard seeds

1 shallot, minced

2 cloves garlic, minced

2 tablespoons sherry vinegar

1 tablespoon Dijon mustard

$1/3$ cup extra virgin olive oil

2 teaspoons chopped fresh fennel greens

Salt

Freshly ground black pepper

3 bulbs fennel, very thinly sliced

1 celeriac, peeled and grated

1 small red onion, julienned

To prepare the dressing: Combine the wine and mustard seeds in a small sauté pan over high heat, and reduce until just about dry. Transfer the mustard seeds to a small bowl, add the shallot, garlic, vinegar, and mustard, and whisk well. While whisking, slowly add the olive oil and whisk until thick and emulsified. Add the fennel greens, mix well, and season to taste with salt and pepper. Set aside. (The dressing can be prepared in advance and kept refrigerated for up to 2 weeks).

To assemble the salad: In a bowl, combine the fennel, celeriac, and red onion. Add the dressing and toss well. Serve chilled or at room temperature.

entrées

Tuscan-Style Roasted Game Hens / 70

Pan-Seared Seabass with Tomato-Saffron
    Broth / 71

Seared Ahi Tuna on Pasta Tossed with
    Asian-Style Pesto / 72

New York Steaks with Kalamata Olive
    Butter / 74

Chicken Breasts Stuffed with Walnut
    Pesto / 76

Roasted Rack of Lamb with Mint Aioli / 78

Phyllo-Wrapped Salmon with Sweet Red
    Pepper Sauce / 80

Grilled Cherry-Marinated Leg of Lamb / 84

Osso Buco with Sundried Tomatoes / 85

John's Famous Barbecued Ribs with Secret
    Cure and Mango Barbecue Sauce / 86

Spice-Rubbed Flank Steak with Pumpkin-
    Pepper Bacon Salad / 87

Corn Dogs / 89

Lobster Salad with Pecan-Mustard
    Dressing / 90

Poached Seabass with Roasted Yellow
    Pepper–Yogurt Sauce / 92

Whole Roasted Beef Tenderloin with Green
    Peppercorn Béarnaise / 94

Monkfish on Avocado Salad with Basil
    Vinaigrette / 96

Veal Stew with Lemon and Fennel / 100

Country Ribs Braised with Chiles / 101

Crab Frittata / 102

Shiitake-Dredged Salmon with Green Onion–
    Mushroom Compote / 103

Chile-Lemongrass Prawns / 105

New York Steaks with Chimichurri and Port
    Glaze / 106

Crown Roast with Roasted Pear and Walnut
    Dressing / 107

Roasted Vegetable Crab Cakes with Red
    Pepper Rouille / 108

Cumin-Roasted Chicken Salad with Roasted
    Jalapeño Dressing / 110

Bistro Steamed Clams with Roasted Shallots
    and Saffron / 114

Grilled Honey-Lemon Chicken / 115

Pork Tenderloin with Spicy Glaze and
    Mango Jam / 116

Roasted Pork Loin with Rosemary-Balsamic
    Glaze / 118

Coconut-Shrimp Stew / 119

TUSCAN-STYLE ROASTED GAME HENS

SERVES 6

Tuscan cooks have a real appreciation for ingredients, often letting a beautiful ingredient speak for itself in a dish. Although Tuscan cuisine is fairly simple, don't let that fool you—it takes a lot of restraint to keep from overworking an ingredient. This recipe is perfect for entertaining. You can prepare the hens and keep them in the roasting pan, covered and refrigerated, for up to 24 hours before cooking.

1 onion, diced

3 stalks celery, diced

2 large carrots, peeled and diced

6 Rock Cornish game hens

2 teaspoons extra virgin olive oil

3 cloves garlic, minced

2 teaspoons minced fresh rosemary

2 teaspoons minced fresh sage

1 teaspoon freshly cracked black pepper

2 teaspoons kosher salt

6 thin slices pancetta

Preheat the oven to 425°. Combine the onion, celery, and carrots in the bottom of a roasting pan. Set the hens on top of the vegetables, and drizzle with the olive oil. In a small bowl, mix together the garlic, rosemary, sage, black pepper, and salt. Rub the herb mixture over the hens until well coated. Lay a piece of pancetta over the breast of each hen, and secure each piece with 2 toothpicks. Roast the hens for 15 minutes. Decrease the temperature to 350°, and continue roasting until the hens reach an internal temperature of 155°, about 45 minutes. Let sit at room temperature for 3 to 4 minutes before serving. Serve warm.

Wine Suggestion: The more refined flavors and quality of a reserve Chianti will showcase these simple roasted hens.

PAN-SEARED SEABASS with TOMATO-SAFFRON BROTH

SERVES 6

The tomato-saffron broth in this recipe is very beautiful and delicate. Make sure you serve it in shallow, light-colored bowls that will set off the color of the broth and ensure that your guests won't miss a single drop.

Tomato-Saffron Broth

2 vine-ripened tomatoes, peeled, seeded, and diced
    (pages 188 and 189)
2 cloves garlic, chopped
$^1/_2$ onion, diced
$^1/_2$ cup dry white wine
1 cup fish stock (page 186)
$^1/_2$ teaspoon crushed saffron threads
2 teaspoons unsalted butter
Salt
Freshly ground black pepper

6 (6-ounce) seabass fillets or other seasonal
    whitefish
Salt
Freshly ground black pepper
2 tablespoons minced fresh basil
1 tablespoon extra virgin olive oil

To prepare the broth: Combine the tomatoes, garlic, onion, and white wine in a saucepan over high heat and reduce until about $^1/_4$ cup of liquid remains. Add the stock and saffron and reduce until about $^1/_2$ cup of liquid remains. Stir in the butter and season to taste with salt and pepper. Keep warm until ready to serve. (The broth can be made in advance and kept refrigerated for up to 2 days.)

To prepare the fish: If the fillets are more than 1 inch thick, preheat the oven to 350°. Season the fillets with salt and pepper, and sprinkle them with the basil. Heat the olive oil in a very large sauté pan over high heat until smoking hot. Add the fillets and sear until brown, 3 to 4 minutes per side. If the fillets are more than 1 inch thick, bake them for 3 to 4 minutes, until just cooked through.

To serve: Place each fillet in a large, shallow bowl and top with the broth. Serve warm.

Wine Suggestion: Pour a Dolcetto and really set this dish on its feet. With a name that means "little sweet one," it's a very fruity wine with slightly sweet tones. The flavors taste wonderful against the slight acidity of the tomato-saffron broth, and they won't overwhelm the seabass.

SEARED AHI TUNA on PASTA TOSSED with ASIAN-STYLE PESTO

I like to serve this pesto-tossed pasta at room temperature, which contrasts nicely with the warm seared tuna. The pesto is great to have on hand during the summer, and it will keep in the refrigerator for up to a week. Instead of tossing it with pasta, you can serve it on top of the seared tuna or on a grilled chicken breast, or mix it with rice or couscous.

Asian-Style Pesto

2 cloves garlic

2 teaspoons peeled, chopped fresh ginger

$^1/_4$ cup coarsely chopped fresh cilantro

$^1/_4$ cup coarsely chopped fresh basil

$^1/_4$ cup coarsely chopped fresh chives

$^1/_2$ cup toasted almonds (page 186)

$^3/_4$ cup freshly grated Parmesan cheese

$^1/_4$ cup vegetable oil

1 teaspoon sesame oil

1 teaspoon dried red chile flakes

1 tablespoon soy sauce

1 pound dried linguine

Salt

6 (6-ounce) ahi tuna steaks

2 tablespoons honey

$^1/_3$ cup soy sauce

1 tablespoon peeled, chopped fresh ginger

2 cloves garlic, chopped

2 tablespoons vegetable oil

To prepare the pesto: Place the garlic, ginger, cilantro, basil, chives, almonds, and cheese in the bowl of a food processor, and process until well blended. With the machine running, add the vegetable oil, sesame oil, chile flakes, and soy sauce through the feed tube, and process until smooth. Set aside, or refrigerate for up to 1 week.

To prepare the pasta: In a stockpot over high heat, bring about 8 cups of salted water to a boil. Add the linguine and cook until al dente, 7 to 10 minutes. Drain well. Place the pasta in a large bowl, add the pesto, and toss well. Season with salt, if needed. Cover with plastic wrap to keep warm.

To sear the tuna: Place the tuna steaks on a large plate. In a small bowl, whisk together the honey, soy sauce, ginger, and garlic. Pour the mixture over the tuna. Heat the vegetable oil in a very large sauté pan over high heat until smoking hot. Add the tuna and sear just until rare, 2 to 3 minutes per side, depending on the thickness of the steaks. (Do not overcook the tuna or it will be too dry.)

To serve: Place the warm pasta on a large serving platter, and top with the tuna steaks. Serve immediately.

Wine Suggestion: When I prepare an Asian dish with complex flavors, I think a dry and slightly fruity Pinot Gris is a match made in heaven.

NEW YORK STEAKS with KALAMATA OLIVE BUTTER

If I'm serving my guests steak, I prefer to serve New York strip over other cuts. It may require a steak knife, but its flavor makes up for it. The olive butter in this recipe can be made in advance and kept refrigerated for up to a week, or frozen for up to six months. Try using it to finish a pasta or risotto dish, or to slather on steamed corn.

Kalamata Olive Butter

1 head roasted garlic (page 185)

1 clove garlic, chopped

1 shallot, chopped

2 anchovy fillets

$^1/_2$ cup pitted kalamata olives

1 teaspoon chopped fresh marjoram

$^1/_3$ cup unsalted butter, diced

Salt

Freshly ground black pepper

6 (8-ounce) New York steaks

Salt

Freshly ground black pepper

1 tablespoon extra virgin olive oil

To prepare the butter: Combine the roasted garlic, fresh garlic, shallot, anchovies, olives, and marjoram in the bowl of a food processor. With the machine running, add the butter, a few pieces at a time, through the feed tube and process until smooth. Scrape down the sides of the bowl, and season to taste with salt and pepper. Spread a foot-long piece of plastic wrap out on the counter. Place the butter in about a 10-inch-long strip down the middle of the plastic wrap, stopping at least 1 inch from each end. Fold one side of the plastic wrap over the butter, and tightly roll up the butter in the excess to form a log. Refrigerate.

To prepare the steaks: Preheat the oven to 350°. Season the steaks with salt and pepper. Heat the olive oil in a very large sauté pan over high heat until smoking hot. Add the steaks and sear well, 2 to 3 minutes per side. Set the pan in the oven, and cook 6 to 8 minutes for medium doneness.

To serve: Place the steaks on a platter or on individual plates, and top each with a $1/2$-inch slice of the olive butter.

Wine Suggestion: A steak just cries out for a robust wine like a Merlot. The bit of tang from the olives makes a nice contrast with the fruitiness of the wine.

CHICKEN BREASTS STUFFED with WALNUT PESTO

I like to serve these with wild rice, because the nutty flavor of the rice complements the pesto. You can stuff the chicken breasts up to two hours ahead of time, then keep them refrigerated until ready to bake.

Walnut Pesto

2 cups walnuts, toasted (page 186)

$^1/_2$ cup freshly grated Asiago or Parmesan cheese

3 cloves garlic

2 teaspoons chopped fresh thyme

1 teaspoon chopped fresh marjoram

$^1/_2$ cup extra virgin olive oil

Salt

Freshly ground black pepper

6 chicken breasts, boned, with the drumstick attached

2 teaspoons extra virgin olive oil

Salt

Freshly ground black pepper

$^1/_4$ cup balsamic syrup (page 189)

To prepare the pesto: In the bowl of a food processor, combine the walnuts, cheese, garlic, thyme, and marjoram, and process until the walnuts are finely ground. With the machine running, slowly add the olive oil and process until smooth. Season to taste with salt and pepper. Transfer the pesto to a pastry bag without a tip. Set aside.

To stuff and bake the chicken breasts: Preheat the oven to 425°. Cut a 1-inch slit in the side of each chicken breast, then move the knife back and forth inside the slit to create a pocket. Place the tip of the pastry bag inside the pocket of the chicken breast, and then squeeze the bag to fill the pocket with pesto. Place the breasts on a well-greased baking sheet, drizzle with the olive oil, and season with salt and pepper. Bake until the chicken reaches an internal temperature of 155°, 15 to 20 minutes.

To serve: Serve warm, drizzled with balsamic syrup.

Wine Suggestion: A medium-bodied Rhône, with its peppery tones and slightly acidic finish, is a wonderful complement to the rich pesto filling.

ROASTED RACK of LAMB with MINT AIOLI

SERVES 4

Mint is a flavor that has traditionally been served with lamb in the form of a neon-green jelly. I decided to do the lamb justice by incorporating the mint into a garlicky aioli instead. Not only does the aioli taste great but also it can be made up to a week in advance. If you really want to be prepared, sear the lamb racks up to four hours ahead of time, then finish them off in the oven just 15 minutes before serving.

Mint Aioli

1 egg yolk

2 cloves garlic

2 tablespoons white wine vinegar

2 teaspoons Dijon mustard

1 cup extra virgin olive oil

1 tablespoon chopped fresh mint

1 teaspoon chopped fresh basil

1 teaspoon green peppercorns

Salt

Freshly ground black pepper

2 racks of lamb (about 14 bones), fat and silver skin removed

2 teaspoons crushed green peppercorns

Salt

1 tablespoon extra virgin olive oil

To prepare the aioli: Place the egg yolk, garlic, vinegar, and mustard in the bowl of a food processor and process until smooth. With the machine running, slowly add the olive oil through the feed tube and process until thick and emulsified. Add the mint, basil, and peppercorns, and process until well blended. Transfer the aioli to a bowl and season to taste with salt and pepper. Refrigerate until ready to serve.

To roast the lamb: Preheat the oven to 325°. Season the lamb with the green peppercorns and salt. Heat the olive oil in a roasting pan set over high heat until smoking hot. Add the lamb racks, meat side down, and sear until very brown, about 3 minutes. Turn and sear for 2 to 3 minutes. Set the pan in the oven and roast the lamb for about 15 minutes for medium-rare doneness. Remove the lamb from the oven and let it sit for about 2 minutes before slicing. Cut the racks into individual chops, slicing between the bones.

To serve: Divide the lamb among 4 individual plates, and drizzle with the aioli. Serve hot, with extra aioli on the side.

NOTE: Children and individuals who are immunosuppressed should not eat uncooked eggs that have not been pasteurized.

Wine Suggestion: Lamb can have a fairly assertive flavor. A full-bodied Merlot with lots of intense fruit can stand up to it while really accentuating the richness of the meat.

PHYLLO-WRAPPED SALMON with SWEET RED PEPPER SAUCE

SERVES 6

Most of this dramatic entrée can be prepared in advance. You can wrap the salmon in the phyllo, place it on a greased baking sheet, cover it with plastic wrap, and refrigerate for up to two hours before baking. The sauce can be made up to a day in advance then reheated just before serving. For variation, stuff the salmon with other fresh herbs or even spice pastes.

Sweet Red Pepper Sauce

1 cup dry white wine

2 cloves garlic, chopped

2 shallots, chopped

2 teaspoons peeled, chopped fresh ginger

4 red bell peppers, seeded and chopped

1 cup chicken stock (page 187) or fish stock (page 186)

2 tablespoons sweet hot chile sauce

Soy sauce

6 (6-ounce) salmon fillets

Salt

Freshly ground black pepper

2 cloves garlic, minced

2 teaspoons peeled, minced fresh ginger

1 tablespoon chopped fresh basil

6 sheets phyllo dough

2 tablespoons unsalted butter, melted

Basil sprigs, for garnish

To prepare the sauce: In a saucepan over high heat, combine the wine, garlic, shallots, and ginger, and reduce by one-half, 5 to 6 minutes. Add the peppers and stock, and cook until the peppers are tender, about 8 minutes. Stir in the chile sauce. Transfer the sauce to the bowl of a food processor and purée until smooth. Season with the soy sauce to taste. Keep warm until ready to serve.

To prepare and bake the salmon: Preheat the oven to 375°. Place the salmon fillets on a baking sheet, season with salt and pepper, and distribute the garlic, ginger, and basil over the tops. Place 1 sheet of phyllo on a flat work surface, and brush lightly with butter. Set 1 fillet about one-third of the way up on the sheet of phyllo. Fold the edge of the phyllo that is closest to you over the fillet. Fold the sides to cover the fillet, then roll the fillet to the end of the dough to form a package. Place the fillet, fold side down, on a well-greased baking sheet. Continue with the remaining fillets and phyllo. Bake until golden brown, about 12 minutes.

To serve: Cut each salmon package in half on the diagonal. Drizzle about 2 tablespoons of the sauce on each plate. Place one half of a package on each plate, then lean the other half against the bottom half, with the cut side facing out. Garnish with a basil sprig. Serve warm.

Wine Suggestion: Salmon has such depth that a lighter-style red, such as Pinot Noir, meshes very well.

How Much Should I Make?

Even the most experienced hosts worry about making too much or too little food. While leftovers can sometimes be great, having too little to serve can be embarrassing. Even after years of working as chefs and cooking in quantity, John and I have a hard time preparing the right amount of food—we always seem to end up with too much! For example, when John makes the gravy for Thanksgiving dinner for just our family, it's not uncommon for him to overestimate by at least a gallon or two. Luckily we don't have a problem calculating amounts for caterings or large parties at home, thanks to a few rules of thumb we keep in mind. Follow these pointers when you're planning your own party, so you'll be right on target.

- **For passed appetizers served before an entire dinner, figure on three per person. If the cocktail hour will be longer than 45 minutes or so, increase the appetizers to four to five per person.**

- **For an appetizer-only party, serve six to eight appetizers per person.**

- **For the entrée course of a sit-down meal, plan to serve 6 to 8 ounces of meat or fish per person.**

- **For a buffet with two entrées (such as a meat and a fish), plan to serve 3 to 4 ounces of each entrée per person.**

COOKING FOR VERY LARGE GROUPS

Cooking for very large groups (say twenty or more people) can be a challenge in a home kitchen. But, while limited oven, stove, counter, and refrigerator space might place boundaries on the menu, preparing dinner and serving it in a timely fashion isn't an impossible feat. If a large party looms on your calendar, take a deep breath and keep the following suggestions in mind:

- **First, don't overwhelm yourself. Sure, an array of complicated dishes will wow your guests, but I strongly recommend avoiding recipes that are hard to execute well for a large group. If ambition gets the better of you, you'll most likely end up in a frenzied state at serving time and the food you've labored over will suffer. So do yourself a favor and focus on preparations that are simple but satisfying.**

- **When considering the menu, make sure that the majority of the dishes you choose won't require last-minute attention, like an elaborate plating presentation or an accompanying sauce that must be made at the last moment. Any specials touches or garnishes that deteriorate quickly, such as spun sugar or even something as simple as a scoop of ice cream, should be saved for a time when serving many people at once isn't so crucial. Prep as much as you can ahead of time.**

- If you're short on oven space, think about using your outdoor grill, even if just to keep a dish warm.

- If you have a second oven or even a warming drawer, warm the plates so the food stays hot while you're serving the meal.

GRILLED CHERRY-MARINATED LEG of LAMB

SERVES 6

This summer dish takes advantage of cherries when they're perfectly ripe and juicy. And since the lamb is boneless, it cooks in only ten minutes—so you don't have to stand over the hot grill for too long. Leg of lamb isn't the most tender cut of meat, but the acidity of the marinade will break down the toughness, and the cherries and herbs infuse the meat with incredible flavor.

Marinade

2 shallots, chopped

3 cloves garlic, chopped

2 cups red wine

1 pound fresh sweet cherries, pitted

2 tablespoons brown sugar

$^1/_4$ cup red wine vinegar

$^1/_4$ cup extra virgin olive oil

2 teaspoons chopped fresh marjoram

2 teaspoons chopped fresh basil

2 teaspoons soy sauce

1 (4- to 5-pound) leg of lamb, fat and silver skin removed

Salt

2 teaspoons freshly cracked black pepper

To prepare the marinade: In a large saucepan over high heat, combine the shallots, garlic, wine, and cherries. Bring the mixture to a boil and reduce until about 1 cup of wine remains. Add the brown sugar and cook, stirring often, 3 to 5 minutes longer. In a food processor or blender, purée the wine mixture. Transfer to a bowl, and whisk in the vinegar, oil, marjoram, basil, and soy sauce. Let cool completely.

To marinate the lamb: Place the lamb in a large bowl and pour the marinade over it. Cover the bowl with plastic wrap, refrigerate, and marinate for at least 1 hour, or up to 12 hours.

To grill the lamb: Oil the grill and heat until very hot (to test, you should be able to hold your hand over the grill for no more than 5 seconds). Season the lamb with salt and pepper, place it on the grill and cook 3 to 4 minutes per side for medium-rare doneness. Slice very thin. Serve hot.

Wine Suggestion: The flavor of the cherries in the marinade marries perfectly with a rich, full-bodied Merlot.

OSSO BUCO with SUNDRIED TOMATOES

SERVES 8

Osso buco is such a comforting and satisfying entrée. It is my favorite dinner to make on a cold winter evening, especially if we're having a dinner party. Osso buco and even lamb shanks can be flavored with just about anything, from fresh herbs to curry—and once it is in the oven, I don't have to worry about a thing for at least an hour.

1 tablespoon extra virgin olive oil

8 (10-ounce) veal shanks

Salt

Freshly ground black pepper

1 cup flour

2 shallots, chopped

1 onion, minced

2 cloves garlic, chopped

2 cups red wine

3 vine-ripened tomatoes, peeled, seeded, and
    chopped (pages 188 and 189)

¼ cup diced oil- or dry-packed sundried tomatoes

6 cups veal stock or chicken stock (page 187),
    brought to a boil

2 teaspoons chopped fresh marjoram

1 tablespoon chopped fresh oregano

2 tablespoons unsalted butter

Salt

Freshly cracked black pepper

To prepare the osso buco: Preheat the oven to 425°. Place the oil in a roasting pan and heat it in the oven until smoking hot. Season the shanks with salt and pepper, then dredge in the flour. Place them in the hot oil, set the pan in the oven, and sear well, 3 to 4 minutes per side. Add the shallots, onion, and garlic, return the pan to the oven, and roast for 3 minutes. Remove the pan from the oven, add the wine, and stir well to deglaze the pan. Return the pan to the oven, and cook the shanks 10 minutes longer. Add the tomatoes, sundried tomatoes, stock, marjoram, and oregano, cover the pan with a lid or foil, lower the oven temperature to 350°, and cook until the shanks are tender, about 50 minutes. Remove the shanks from the stock and transfer to a serving platter. Skim and discard the fat from the surface of the stock. Set the roasting pan over high heat and boil the stock for about 5 minutes to reduce. Whisk in the butter and season to taste with salt and cracked pepper.

To serve: Pour the sauce over the shanks on the platter. Serve immediately.

Wine Suggestion: The broth in this dish is light but intensely flavorful, and I think a white wine would be blown away. Instead, try a Pinot Noir to match the flavors of the sundried tomatoes and the herbs.

JOHN'S FAMOUS BARBECUED RIBS with SECRET CURE and MANGO BARBECUE SAUCE

SERVES 12

When we have a barbecue at our house, John always makes his famous ribs. Our friend Marianne calls John's cure "The Drug Rub," because after we eat a big pile of ribs, we become very lethargic. You will have more of the cure than you need; keep it to use on steak, chicken, and even salmon. It will keep in an airtight container for up to six months.

Secret Cure

2 cups brown sugar

1 cup kosher salt

3 tablespoons ground mace

3 tablespoons ground allspice

3 tablespoons onion powder

3 tablespoons garlic powder

1 1/2 tablespoons ground cloves

Mango Barbecue Sauce

1/4 cup freshly squeezed lime juice

2 cups hoisin sauce

1/2 cup frozen orange juice concentrate, thawed

1/2 cup tomato paste

1/2 cup sweet soy sauce, or 1/2 cup soy sauce and
    1/4 cup honey

1 cup seedless tamarind paste

1/2 cup mango purée

10 pounds baby back ribs, membrane removed

To prepare the cure: In the bowl of a food processor, combine all the cure ingredients and process until well blended.

To prepare the barbecue sauce: In a large bowl, whisk together all of the sauce ingredients. Refrigerate until ready to use, or for up to 2 weeks.

To cure the ribs: Rub the ribs generously with the cure, then refrigerate for 24 hours.

To grill the ribs: Oil the grill. If using a charcoal grill, place the charcoal on one side of the barbecue, and light; if using a gas grill, turn on only one element and heat until very hot (to test, you should be able to hold your hand over the grill for no more than 5 seconds). Gently rinse the excess cure off of the ribs. Place the ribs on the unlit side of the grill. Cover and cook for 2 hours. Place the ribs over the hot coals or element and baste with the barbecue sauce. Grill 20 to 30 minutes longer, or until tender, basting about every 10 minutes.

To serve: Cut the ribs into 2-rib segments. Serve warm.

Wine Suggestion: I like to pour Zinfandel with these ribs. There's a lot happening in this dish, so a wine with the same backbone is in order. The only other beverage I would suggest would be a cold local microbrew.

SPICE-RUBBED FLANK STEAK with PUMPKIN-PEPPER BACON SALAD

SERVES 6

The spice rub is tasty on all types of meat and on chicken, so you may want to double the rub recipe (it will keep in an airtight container for up to six months). The pumpkin salad can be made a day in advance and warmed just before serving. Any leftover steak makes a great sandwich.

Spice Rub

1 tablespoon kosher salt

3 tablespoons brown sugar

2 teaspoons ground cumin

1 teaspoon ground coriander

1 teaspoon chile powder

2 teaspoons dried oregano

1 teaspoon dried thyme

1 teaspoon dried mustard

$1/2$ teaspoon cayenne pepper

1 (3-pound) flank steak

2 teaspoons extra virgin olive oil

Pumpkin-Pepper Bacon Salad

6 slices pepper bacon, diced

2 teaspoons extra virgin olive oil

4 cups peeled, diced pumpkin or other squash, such as butternut

1 onion, cut into large dice

2 tablespoon sherry vinegar

2 cloves garlic, chopped

1 teaspoon Dijon mustard

2 teaspoons chopped fresh oregano

$1/2$ teaspoon freshly cracked black pepper

Salt

continued

To prepare the spice rub: Combine all of the rub ingredients in a bowl and mix well.

To cure the steak: Generously coat the steak with the rub. Cover, refrigerate, and let it cure for 4 to 6 hours. Lightly rinse the cured steak under running water to remove excess rub. Set on a plate and refrigerate, uncovered, until ready to cook.

To prepare the salad: Preheat the oven to 375°. Heat a very large ovenproof sauté pan over high heat until very hot. Add the diced bacon and cook until crispy. Remove the bacon from the pan, reserving the drippings in the pan, and drain on paper towels. Set aside. Add the olive oil to the drippings in the pan and heat until smoking hot. Add the pumpkin and cook, without stirring, until brown, about 4 minutes. Toss and repeat. Add the onions, set the pan in the oven, and cook until the pumpkin is tender, about 15 minutes. Remove from the oven, add the vinegar, garlic, mustard, oregano, and pepper, and mix well. Season to taste with salt. Add the bacon to the salad and mix well. Keep warm until ready to serve.

To grill the steak: Oil the grill and heat until very hot (to test, you should be able to hold your hand over the grill for no more than 5 seconds). Grill the steak for 3 to 4 minutes per side for medium-rare doneness. Let the steak sit for about 2 minutes, then slice very thin across the grain at about a 45-degree angle.

To serve: Distribute the warm salad among 6 plates, and top with slices of steak.

Wine Suggestion: I like to pour a full-bodied Zinfandel with this dish. The peppery salad and the spice mixture call for a wine that will stand up to the complicated flavors and still let the sweetness of the pumpkin shine through.

CORN DOGS

SERVES 8

I may have used the children's birthday party menu as an excuse to include this recipe in the book, but I have to admit it's also for me! You can prepare the batter about an hour ahead of time and have the dogs skewered and ready to go. Keep the corn dogs warm in a 250° oven until you're ready to serve. Be sure to make a few extras for the grownups.

Cornmeal Batter

1 cup cornmeal

2 cups flour

1 tablespoon sugar

1 teaspoon baking soda

2 cups buttermilk

4 eggs, separated

1 teaspoon kosher salt

Vegetable oil, for deep-frying

8 good-quality hot dogs

Mustard and ketchup, as accompaniments

To prepare the batter: In a bowl, combine the cornmeal, flour, sugar, and baking soda, and mix well. In another bowl, whisk together the buttermilk and egg yolks until smooth. Slowly pour the egg mixture into the dry ingredients and mix well. Add the salt and mix well. In the bowl of a heavy-duty mixer, whip the egg whites at high speed until they hold soft peaks. Gently fold the egg whites into the batter. Set aside.

To fry the corn dogs: Heat 6 inches of oil in a wide saucepan over high heat until it reaches 350°. Insert a stick into one end of each hot dog.

Dredge the hot dogs in the batter and place as many as will fit in the pan of hot oil. Do not overcrowd. Cook until golden brown, about 6 minutes. Drain on paper towels and hold in a warm oven. Continue with the remaining hot dogs and batter. Serve warm with ketchup and mustard.

Beverage suggestion: A glass of wine and a corn dog just don't seem to go together. A corn dog in one hand and a beer in the other? Now you're talking. But just because it's a corn dog doesn't mean you should drink the King of Beers—instead, I'd suggest a micro-brewed hefeweizen.

LOBSTER SALAD with PECAN-MUSTARD DRESSING

SERVES 4

This luncheon salad is perfect for those times when you want to keep the meal fairly simple, yet dress it up a bit. I first made it when I hosted a friend's bridal shower. I wanted the luncheon to be elegant, but I had to act as host, cook, and entertainment coordinator at the same time. If lobster is a bit too fancy or is out of season, try fresh local crabmeat or even a grilled chicken breast.

Pecan-Mustard Dressing

2 tablespoons white wine vinegar

1 tablespoon grated lemon zest

1 tablespoon lemon juice

2 cloves garlic, chopped

1 egg yolk

2 teaspoons Dijon mustard

1 teaspoon whole-grain mustard

1 teaspoon chopped fresh thyme

$^1/_2$ cup pecan oil or extra virgin olive oil

Salt

Freshly ground black pepper

Lobster Salad

1 head romaine lettuce, rinsed, spun dry, and torn into smaller pieces

$^1/_2$ pound *haricots verts* or other seasonal green beans, blanched and shocked (page 188)

2 large vine-ripened tomatoes, peeled, seeded, and chopped (pages 188 and 189)

2 (2-pound) lobsters, cooked and meat removed (page 186)

1 small red onion, sliced thinly into rounds

$^1/_2$ cup chopped toasted pecans (page 186)

$^3/_4$ cup toasted garlic bread crumbs (page 185)

To prepare the dressing: Combine the vinegar, lemon zest and juice, garlic, egg yolk, mustards, and thyme in the bowl of a food processor. With the machine running, slowly add the oil and process until thick and emulsified. Season to taste with salt and pepper. Refrigerate until ready to serve, or up to 1 week.

To assemble and serve the salad: Place the lettuce in a large bowl. Add the dressing and toss well. Divide the salad among 4 large plates, then add the *haricots verts,* tomatoes, and lobster. Top with the red onion slices. Sprinkle with the pecans and bread crumbs. Serve cold.

NOTE: Children and individuals who are immunosuppressed should not eat uncooked eggs that have not been pasteurized.

Wine Suggestion: Dry Chenin Blanc is a lively wine that won't be overwhelmed by the mustard in the dressing, yet it has a delicate floral quality that showcases the sweet, rich lobster.

POACHED SEABASS with ROASTED YELLOW PEPPER–YOGURT SAUCE

SERVES 8

This sauce tastes just as wonderful if made with sweet red bell peppers instead of yellow peppers, and you can make it a few days in advance if it's kept tightly covered and refrigerated. The fish comes together very quickly, but if you'd rather spend the time with your guests, have the fish ready in the pan a couple of hours ahead of time and refrigerate until you're ready to bake it.

Roasted Yellow Pepper–Yogurt Sauce

4 yellow peppers, roasted, peeled, seeded, and diced (page 186)

$^1/_2$ cup plain yogurt

2 cloves garlic, chopped

1 tablespoon peeled, chopped fresh ginger

$^1/_2$ teaspoon five-spice powder

1 teaspoon ground cumin

1 teaspoon ground coriander

$^1/_4$ teaspoon cayenne pepper

Salt

Freshly ground black pepper

8 (6-ounce) seabass fillets

Salt

Freshly ground black pepper

2 tablespoons unsalted butter

1 cup white wine

$^1/_2$ cup fish stock (page 186) or chicken stock (page 187)

2 shallots, chopped

2 cloves garlic, chopped

1 cinnamon stick

To prepare the sauce: Purée the peppers in a food processor or blender until smooth. Add the yogurt, garlic, ginger, five-spice powder, cumin, coriander, and cayenne, and purée until smooth. Transfer the mixture to a bowl, and season to taste with salt and pepper. Refrigerate until ready to serve.

To poach the fish: Preheat the oven to 350°. Place the fish in a roasting pan and season with salt and pepper. Top with the butter, wine, stock, shallots, garlic, and cinnamon stick. Bake until the fish is just cooked through, about 12 minutes. Remove the fish from the poaching liquid, discarding the liquid.

To serve: Place the fish on a serving platter, and drizzle with the yogurt sauce. Serve hot, with extra sauce on the side.

Wine Suggestion: The spiciness of a dry Gewürztraminer deliciously complements the touch of sweetness and the warm spices in the sauce, and the combination will dazzle your guests.

WHOLE ROASTED BEEF TENDERLOIN with GREEN PEPPERCORN BÉARNAISE

SERVES 12

Cooking a whole beef tenderloin is not something you would do every day, so serve it when you want to pull out all the stops. By first searing and then roasting the beef, you'll end up with the juiciest piece of meat. Béarnaise sauce, like the little black dress, is a classic that never goes out of style. In this version, I've added green peppercorns to give it just a bit of spice.

1 (5- to 6-pound) whole beef tenderloin, fat and
　　silver skin removed
Kosher salt
2 tablespoons chopped fresh basil
$^1/_2$ teaspoon freshly cracked black peppercorns
2 tablespoons extra virgin olive oil

Green Peppercorn Béarnaise
1 cup white wine
1 shallot, chopped
2 cloves garlic, chopped
1 tablespoon chopped fresh tarragon
$^1/_4$ cup tarragon vinegar
1 teaspoon grated lemon zest
4 egg yolks
2 teaspoons crushed green peppercorns
1 cup unsalted butter
Salt
Freshly ground black pepper

To roast the tenderloin: Preheat the oven to 425°. Season the tenderloin with the salt, basil, and cracked black pepper. Place the olive oil in a roasting pan and heat it in the oven until smoking hot. Add the tenderloin, place the pan in the oven, and sear the tenderloin well on all sides, 5 to 7 minutes. Lower the oven temperature to 300° and roast the tenderloin until it reaches an internal temperature of 135° to 140° for medium-rare doneness, about 30 minutes. When the tenderloin is done, remove it from the oven and let it sit for about 4 minutes before slicing.

To prepare the béarnaise: While the meat is roasting, combine the wine, shallot, garlic, tarragon, vinegar, and lemon zest in a heavy saucepan over high heat, and reduce until about $1/4$ cup of liquid remains. Let cool completely. Transfer the mixture to the top of a double boiler and whisk in the egg yolks and crushed peppercorns. Cook the mixture, stirring often, until it thickens to the consistency of softly whipped cream, 3 to 5 minutes. Meanwhile, melt the butter in a saucepan over low heat. Remove the egg mixture from the heat and slowly whisk in the butter. Season to taste with salt and pepper. Keep warm until ready to serve.

To serve: Place the tenderloin slices on a large platter, and top with about half of the béarnaise. Serve hot, with the remaining sauce on the side.

Wine Suggestion: An aged Cabernet Sauvignon with a bit of softness will complement the richness of this classic dish.

MONKFISH on AVOCADO SALAD with BASIL VINAIGRETTE

SERVES 4

With the sweet flavor and dense texture of monkfish, it's no surprise that it used to be known as poor man's lobster. If monkfish is un-available or is not in season, try another firm whitefish, such as seabass. The presentation of this dish can be very showy. Fan the slices of monkfish over the top of the salad, and then drizzle with the vinaigrette. I like to put the vinaigrette in a squirt bottle—it gives me more control so I can drizzle the dressing exactly where I want it.

Avocado Salad

$1/2$ cup minced red onion

1 clove garlic, chopped

Grated zest and juice of 1 lime

1 teaspoon cayenne sauce

1 large avocado, peeled and diced

Salt

Freshly ground black pepper

Basil Vinaigrette

2 tablespoons sherry vinegar

1 shallot, minced

1 clove garlic, chopped

2 tablespoons chopped fresh basil

$1/3$ cup extra virgin olive oil

$1/2$ teaspoon ground cumin

Salt

Freshly ground black pepper

$1^1/2$ to 2 pounds monkfish fillet, membrane removed

Salt

Freshly ground black pepper

1 teaspoon ground cumin

$1/2$ teaspoon ground coriander

$1/2$ teaspoon chile powder

1 tablespoon extra virgin olive oil

To prepare the salad: Combine the onion, garlic, lime zest and juice, cayenne sauce, and avocado in a bowl, and mix well. Season to taste with salt and pepper. Cover and refrigerate.

To prepare the vinaigrette: Whisk together the vinegar, shallot, garlic, and basil in a bowl. While whisking, slowly add the olive oil and whisk until thickened and emulsified. Add the cumin, season to taste with salt and pepper, and whisk well. Set aside.

To prepare the fish: Preheat the oven to 375°. Season the fish with salt, pepper, cumin, coriander, and chile powder. Heat the olive oil in a large, ovenproof sauté pan over high heat until smoking hot. Add the fish and sear well on all sides, 6 to 8 minutes total. Set the pan in the oven and bake the fish until just cooked through, about 8 minutes. Slice very thin.

To serve: Place a heaping $1/4$ cup of the salad in the middle of 4 individual plates. Top with the slices of fish, and drizzle with the vinaigrette. Serve immediately.

Wine Suggestion: Sauvignon Blanc tastes just right with this salad. Look for one with a citrus or grapefruit element—it will be very complementary to the fresh, bright flavors of the salad and the touch of sweetness of the monkfish.

Tips for Serving Wine

There's no reason to be intimidated by serving wine, even if you're a novice. Wine is meant to be enjoyed and shared with others, so don't get caught up in all the jargon, old-fashioned rules, and opinions. White wine with fish, red wine with meat used to be the hard-and-fast rule. Thankfully, over the last fifteen to twenty years, people have become more experimental with wine pairing, stepping outside those strict boundaries.

No matter what anyone says, my primary rule is this: Drink only what you truly enjoy, not what someone else dictates. What's the fun of preparing a fabulous dinner only to have it spoiled by a bottle of wine you and your guests don't enjoy? To account for my guests' varied tastes, I will sometimes offer two or even three wines at dinner.

For each entrée recipe in this book, I suggest a wine that I think goes particularly well with the dish, and I explain why I think the specific varietal is a good match. But please, experiment and find your own pairings, if mine don't suit your taste.

Both the experienced wine drinker and the novice can find something useful in these tips:

- **Use clean wineglasses, and that means clean of soap residue, too. Hand-wash wineglasses and dry them with a cotton towel while they're still warm.**

- **Have a good corkscrew. My favorite is the waiter's key—compact and simple to use, it will never fail you.**

- **Serve red wines no warmer than 67°. Sometimes this means chilling a bottle in the refrigerator for a while. If served too warm, red wines can lose their bright fruit aroma.**

- **White wines should be served no colder than 43°, so a bottle may have to sit at room temperature until it comes to the proper temperature. White wines that are too cold lose both their aroma and their complex flavors.**

- **Keep an ice bucket handy for quickly chilling white wine or for keeping Champagne cold while serving.**

- There are wineglasses shaped specifically for red, white, sparkling, and dessert wines. But if you want to have just one type of wineglass in your cupboard, I suggest a large, tulip-shaped one. It makes an ideal all-purpose glass.

- No wine cellar? Don't worry; you can properly store wine in any cool, dark place with a fairly consistent temperature, such as a closet or basement. Keep the bottles on their sides or upside down in a box so the corks will stay moist. If bottles are stored for too long standing up, the corks can dry out, letting in air that will oxidize the wine.

VEAL STEW with LEMON and FENNEL

Most people probably think of stew as better suited for a Sunday night supper than a dinner party, but I think it can be perfect for entertaining. I love to make this cozy dish when we have friends and their kids visiting. Since it requires absolutely no last-minute fuss, I can make it earlier in the day (or even up to two days in advance) and then simply put it on to simmer before everyone arrives.

2^1/$_2$ pounds veal stew meat

Salt

Freshly ground pepper

1 cup flour

2 tablespoons extra virgin olive oil

3 cloves garlic, chopped

1 onion, diced

2 bulbs fennel, cut into large dice

4 Yukon Gold potatoes, diced

6 cups veal or chicken stock (page 187)

Grated zest and juice of 1 lemon

1 tablespoon chopped fresh thyme

2 teaspoons chopped fresh fennel greens

Preheat the oven to 350°. Season the veal with salt and pepper, then dredge in the flour. Heat the olive oil in a Dutch oven or large oven-proof stockpot over high heat until smoking hot. Add the veal and sear well, about 5 minutes. Add the garlic, onion, and fennel and cook for 2 minutes. Add the potatoes, stock, lemon zest and juice, thyme, and fennel greens. Bring to a boil, cover the pan with a lid, and place it in the oven. Cook until the veal is tender, about 40 minutes. Season the stew well with salt and pepper. Serve warm.

Wine Suggestion: A light, fruity Pinot Noir is a great choice for this dish: It will taste wonderful without overpowering the delicate veal.

COUNTRY RIBS BRAISED with CHILES

Country ribs (also known as pork short ribs) have more meat on them than baby back ribs, but they also have more fat. Since they're a tougher cut of meat, they're ideal for braising. In this dish I braise them with chiles, cinnamon, and herbs to infuse them with flavors of Mexico and create a tender, spicy dish. Preparing a braised dish is a real lifesaver when entertaining. Once the food is in the oven, it doesn't require much attention—and it won't fail if you happen to overcook it just a bit.

1 tablespoon extra virgin olive oil

6 to 8 pounds pork short ribs

1 yellow onion, diced

3 cloves garlic, chopped

1 pound Anaheim chiles, roasted, peeled, seeded, and
    diced (page 186)

4 dried ancho chiles, roasted and pulverized
    (page 186)

1 cinnamon stick

4 cups chicken stock (page 187)

2 teaspoons chopped fresh marjoram

1 tablespoon chopped fresh cilantro

Salt

Freshly ground black pepper

Preheat the oven to 350°. Heat the olive oil in a large roasting pan over high heat until smoking hot. Add the ribs and sear well, about 3 minutes per side. Add the onion and garlic, and sauté for 2 minutes. Add the chiles, cinnamon stick, stock, marjoram, and cilantro, and bring to a boil. Cover the pan with a lid or foil, place it in the oven, and braise the ribs until tender, about 40 minutes. Remove the ribs from the oven. Skim the excess fat from the surface of the sauce, and discard. Season the sauce to taste with salt and pepper, and pour it back over the ribs. Serve hot.

Wine Suggestion: Chiles and more chiles need a very full-bodied wine like a Zinfandel—or a cold beer—to clear the palate and get you ready for the next bite.

CRAB FRITTATA

SERVES 8

A frittata may sound like a breakfast or brunch item, but it also makes a perfect dinner entrée for casual get-togethers. It's much easier to prepare than individual omelettes, which require you to stand at the stove as you make each one. When I serve a frittata, I slide it onto a large platter and then cut it into wedges, making serving a breeze. If you don't have all of the ingredients on hand, you can always modify the recipe with leftovers.

1 tablespoon extra virgin olive oil

1 small onion, diced

2 cloves garlic, chopped

1 pound asparagus, cut on the diagonal into $1/2$-inch-long pieces

2 vine-ripened tomatoes, peeled, seeded, and diced (pages 188 and 189)

$1/2$ bunch spinach, rinsed well and spun dry

1 pound Dungeness crabmeat or other local crabmeat, drained well

10 eggs, beaten

1 tablespoon chopped fresh tarragon

6 dashes Tabasco sauce

Salt

Freshly ground black pepper

$1/2$ cup grated or sliced fontina cheese

$1/2$ cup sour cream, for garnish

Lemon zest, for garnish

Tarragon sprigs, for garnish

Preheat the oven to 350°. Heat the olive oil in a 12-inch ovenproof nonstick sauté pan over high heat until very hot. Add the onion and garlic, and sauté for 2 minutes. Add the asparagus and sauté just until crisp-tender, about 4 minutes. Add the tomatoes, spinach, and crabmeat, and cook just until the spinach wilts. Pour in the eggs and sprinkle with the tarragon and Tabasco. Season with salt and pepper. Using a rubber spatula, gently lift the side of the frittata to allow more of the egg mixture to get to the bottom of the pan. Cook just until the eggs start to set, about 5 minutes. Set the pan in the oven, and bake the frittata for 8 minutes. Sprinkle the cheese on top of the frittata and continue baking until the cheese melts and the eggs are set, about 5 minutes longer. Let cool about 3 minutes before slicing.

Serve warm, topped with sour cream and garnished with lemon zest and a sprig of tarragon.

Wine Suggestion: Pinot Blanc has a very fresh flavor, with just a hint of apple and some sweetness. It really highlights the delicate flavor of the crab.

SHIITAKE-DREDGED SALMON with GREEN ONION— MUSHROOM COMPOTE

SERVES 6

I was lucky enough to have the honor to cook with Julia Child, Anne Willan, Martin Yan, and Graham Kerr here in Portland. This salmon dish is very similar to the one I cooked onstage, and now it's a favorite with friends at home. The most unique part of the recipe is the shiitake flour, which lends an earthy quality to the salmon. I like to serve this in the fall as a wonderful way to show off the abundant mushrooms.

Green Onion-Mushroom Compote

1 tablespoon vegetable oil

2 cloves garlic, chopped

2 teaspoons peeled, chopped fresh ginger

4 cups sliced fresh shiitake mushrooms

$^1/_4$ cup sake or dry white wine

1 bunch green onions, both green and white parts, sliced thinly on the diagonal

1 tablespoon rice vinegar

2 tablespoons soy sauce

Pinch dried red chile flakes, or more to taste

6 (6-ounce) salmon fillets

Salt

Freshly ground black pepper

1 cup dried shiitake mushrooms, ground to a powder in a coffee grinder

2 tablespoons vegetable oil

continued

To prepare the compote: Heat the oil in a large sauté pan over high heat until very hot. Add the garlic and ginger and sauté for 1 minute. Add the mushrooms and sauté until tender, 3 to 4 minutes. Add the sake and cook until the liquid has reduced and the mixture is dry, 3 to 4 minutes. Transfer to a bowl and let cool for about 10 minutes. Add the green onions, vinegar, soy sauce, and red pepper flakes, and mix well. Let cool to room temperature.

To prepare the salmon: Preheat the oven to 350°. Season the salmon fillets with salt and pepper, and then dredge them in the mushroom powder. Heat the oil in a large sauté pan over high heat until smoking hot. Add as many fillets as will fit without overcrowding and sear well, 2 to 3 minutes per side. Transfer the fillets to a lightly oiled baking sheet and sear the remaining fillets. Place the fillets in the oven and bake until just cooked through, 6 to 8 minutes, depending on the thickness of the salmon. Serve hot with the room-temperature mushroom compote.

Wine Suggestion: I like to serve Pinot Noir with this dish. Choose one that is medium-bodied—it will be rich enough to complement the earthy mushrooms, but it won't dominate the fish.

CHILE-LEMONGRASS PRAWNS

SERVES 6

This dish cooks very quickly, so it's important to keep a handle on how fast the prawns are cooking and make sure they remain tender. When prawns are overcooked, they become tough and rubbery—and you should never have to use a knife on a prawn! I seat all of my guests and have John start to pour the wine before I begin cooking this dish. That way I serve tender prawns every time.

1 tablespoon vegetable oil

1 tablespoon peeled, chopped fresh ginger

3 cloves garlic, chopped

2 shallots, chopped

36 prawns (16 to 20 count), peeled and deveined

$^1/_2$ cup mirin wine

2 tablespoons very finely minced lemongrass

$^1/_2$ cup chicken stock or shrimp stock
    (page 187)

$^1/_4$ cup sweet hot chile sauce

Soy sauce

Mark's Jungle Rice (page 24), as an accompaniment

Heat the vegetable oil in a very large sauté pan or wok over high heat until very hot. Add the ginger, garlic, and shallots, and sauté for 1 minute. Add the prawns and cook just until they start to turn pink, 2 to 3 minutes. Add the mirin and lemongrass, and cook, stirring often, 2 to 3 minutes longer. Add the stock and chile sauce, and cook until the prawns are just cooked through. Season to taste with soy sauce. Serve warm with Mark's Jungle Rice.

Wine Suggestion: The spicy tones in Gewürztraminer are a natural with this chile-infused dish. Look for one that is dry or bone-dry; otherwise the wine will be too sweet with the prawns.

NEW YORK STEAKS with CHIMICHURRI and PORT GLAZE

SERVES 4

Chimichurri, a staple of Argentinean cuisine, is a pestolike sauce traditionally served with meat dishes. It can dress up a simple piece of grilled meat, fish, or chicken, adding a punch of flavor and heat. You can make it ahead and keep it refrigerated for up to a month.

Chimichurri

12 cloves garlic, minced

$^1/_2$ cup minced parsley

1 tablespoon chopped fresh oregano

$^1/_2$ small onion, finely minced

1 teaspoon dried red chile flakes

Grated zest and juice of 1 lemon

2 tablespoons red wine vinegar

1 cup extra virgin olive oil

1 teaspoon ground cumin

$^1/_2$ teaspoon freshly cracked black pepper

1 teaspoon kosher salt

Port Glaze

1 (750 milliliter) bottle ruby port

4 (6-ounce) New York steaks

Salt

Freshly ground black pepper

1 tablespoon extra virgin olive oil

To prepare the chimichurri: Place all of the ingredients in a bowl and mix well. Refrigerate until ready to use.

To prepare the port glaze: Heat the port in a heavy saucepan over medium-low heat and reduce until it is thick and syrupy and about $^1/_4$ cup remains. Keep warm until ready to serve, or refrigerate up to 2 days and reheat in the top of a double boiler or in the microwave.

To prepare the steaks: Preheat the oven to 350°. Season the steaks with salt and pepper. In a large ovenproof sauté pan over high heat, heat the olive oil until smoking hot. Add the steaks and sear well, about 3 minutes per side. Place the pan of steaks in the oven and cook for 4 to 6 minutes for medium doneness.

To serve: Place the steaks on individual plates, top with about 1 tablespoon of the chimichurri, and drizzle with the port glaze. Serve hot.

Wine Suggestion: A full-bodied Cabernet Sauvignon will stand up to the garlic and spices of the chimichurri and complement the New York steak.

CROWN ROAST with ROASTED PEAR and WALNUT DRESSING

SERVES 10

A crown roast makes such an elegant presentation. Set the roast on a beautiful tray, have your guests seated at the table, and then carry in your masterpiece as you are lauded with compliments! Of course, this dish is not something you put together at a moment's notice, but you can prepare the stuffing up to two days in advance. It is very important not to stuff the roast until right before cooking.

Roasted Pear and Walnut Dressing

1 tablespoon extra virgin olive oil

3 cloves garlic, chopped

1 onion, diced

3 pears, peeled, cored, and diced

$^1/_2$ cup dry sherry

$^1/_2$ cup pear brandy

4 cups diced French bread

$^1/_2$ cup toasted walnuts (page 186), coarsely chopped

2 teaspoons chopped fresh marjoram

2 teaspoons chopped fresh thyme

1 cup chicken stock (page 187)

3 eggs, lightly beaten

Salt

Freshly ground black pepper

1 (7-pound) crown roast (about 12 bones)

Salt

Freshly ground black pepper

To prepare the dressing: Heat the olive oil in a large sauté pan over high heat until hot. Add the garlic and onion and sauté for 3 to 4 minutes. Add the pears and sauté for about 1 minute. Add the sherry and brandy, and cook until the liquid has reduced and the mixture is dry, 3 to 4 minutes. Transfer the mixture to a large bowl and let cool completely. Add the bread, walnuts, marjoram, and thyme, and toss well. Add the stock and eggs, and mix well. Season with salt and pepper.

To prepare the roast: Preheat the oven to 425°. Place the roast in a roasting pan, season with salt and pepper, and fill the center with the dressing. Roast for 15 minutes, then lower the temperature to 350° and continue roasting until the meat reaches an internal temperature of 145°, about 1$^1/_2$ hours. Remove the roast from the oven and let sit for 5 minutes. Scoop the dressing out into a bowl. Cut the roast into individual chops. Serve warm with the dressing.

Wine Suggestion: Pork is a lighter flavored meat that will get lost in a heavy red wine, so with this dish I like to pour a softer one, like Pinot Noir. The roasting deepens the flavor of the pork, and the warm notes of the wine will complement it beautifully.

ROASTED VEGETABLE CRAB CAKES with RED PEPPER ROUILLE

SERVES 6

I like to serve crab cakes as a first course or as the main focus of a more casual dinner. You can put them together earlier in the day and then fry them right before serving. Rouille makes a perfect match with the crab cakes, but once you taste it you'll also want to have it on hand to top on omelets, drizzle on soups and stews, or serve as a dip for flatbread. It will keep, refrigerated, for several days.

Red Pepper Rouille

2 red bell peppers, roasted, peeled, and seeded (page 186)

2 cloves garlic

2 anchovy fillets, packed in salt or oil

2 slices French bread, crusts removed

2 teaspoons freshly squeezed lemon juice

$^1/_4$ cup extra virgin olive oil

Salt

Freshly ground black pepper

Roasted Vegetable Crab Cakes

1 head fennel, diced

3 shallots, quartered

6 cloves garlic, peeled

2 small Yukon Gold potatoes, peeled and quartered

$^1/_4$ cup plus 1 tablespoon extra virgin olive oil

$1^1/_2$ pounds Dungeness crabmeat or other local crabmeat

1 egg, lightly beaten

$^1/_2$ cup béchamel sauce (page 189), cooled

2 teaspoons chopped fresh thyme

2 teaspoons chopped fresh fennel greens

Salt

Freshly ground black pepper

1 cup flour

To prepare the rouille: Combine the peppers, garlic, anchovies, and French bread in the bowl of a food processor, and process until well blended. With the machine running, add the lemon juice and olive oil through the feed tube, and process until smooth. Season to taste with salt and pepper. Transfer the rouille to a bowl and set aside or refrigerate for up to 1 week.

To roast the vegetables: Preheat the oven to 375°. Place the fennel, shallots, garlic, and potatoes in a roasting pan and drizzle with ¼ cup of the olive oil. Roast the vegetables until tender, about 40 minutes. Let cool completely.

To assemble the crab cakes: Coarsely chop the vegetables and place in a bowl. Add the crabmeat, egg, béchamel sauce, thyme, and fennel greens, and mix well. Season well with salt and pepper. Form the mixture into 12 patties.

To fry the crab cakes: Heat the remaining 1 tablespoon olive oil in a large sauté pan over high heat until smoking hot. Dredge the patties in the flour. Place as many patties as will fit in the pan, and brown each side for 3 to 4 minutes. Repeat with remaining patties. Serve warm, with the rouille on the side.

Wine Suggestion: A crisp, cold Pinot Gris with a bit of forward fruit will contrast with the intensity of the crab and the slight sweetness of the roasted vegetables.

CUMIN-ROASTED CHICKEN SALAD with ROASTED JALAPEÑO DRESSING

SERVES 6

This dish explodes with flavor and texture, so much so that your friends will not be disappointed when you serve them nothing but a salad for dinner! In the summer I serve entrée salads to my friends quite a bit. I don't have to heat up an already hot kitchen, plus composed salads such as this one naturally lend themselves to a lovely presentation.

Cumin-Roasted Chicken

2 teaspoons ground cumin

1 teaspoon ground coriander

1 teaspoon chile powder

Kosher salt

Freshly ground black pepper

6 chicken breasts, bone in

Roasted Jalapeño Dressing

3 jalapeños, roasted, peeled, seeded, and minced (page 186)

2 cloves garlic, chopped

1 shallot, chopped

2 tablespoons rice vinegar

Grated zest and juice of 2 limes

$^3/_4$ cup extra virgin olive oil

2 teaspoons chopped fresh cilantro

1 teaspoon chopped fresh basil

Salt

Freshly ground black pepper

1 pound mesclun mix, rinsed and spun dry

2 vine-ripened tomatoes, quartered

1 red pepper, julienned

$^1/_3$ cup pumpkin seeds, toasted (page 186)

$^1/_2$ cup crumbled queso fresco or feta cheese

To prepare the chicken: Preheat the oven to 350°. In a small bowl, mix together the cumin, coriander, chile powder, and salt and pepper. Loosen the skin of the chicken breasts and rub the meat with the spice mixture. Place in a roasting pan and roast until the chicken is cooked through, about 15 minutes. Let cool for about 10 minutes. Remove and discard the skin, and shred the meat. Set aside. (The chicken can be roasted in advance and kept refrigerated for up to 2 days.)

To prepare the dressing: In a bowl, whisk together the jalapeños, garlic, shallot, vinegar, and lime zest and juice. While whisking, slowly add the olive oil and whisk until the dressing is thick and emulsified. Whisk in the cilantro and basil. Season to taste with salt and pepper. Set aside. (The dressing can be prepared in advance and kept refrigerated for up to 2 weeks.)

To assemble the salads: Arrange the greens, tomatoes, and sweet pepper on 6 individual plates. Top with the chicken, and sprinkle with the pumpkin seeds and cheese. Drizzle with the dressing. Serve immediately.

Wine Suggestion: Since salads usually have vinegar in the dressing, they can be hard entrées to pair with a wine. I suggest a Pinot Gris for this dish; it won't overpower the greens, and it will cool your palate after the chiles.

Five Drinks without the Fire but with All the Sizzle:

NONALCOHOLIC DRINKS

Not every guest will want wine or a cocktail, nor does every occasion call for alcoholic beverages. When you want to offer something more creative than mineral water or a soda, mix up one of these. For the best, most refreshing drinks, be sure to use freshly squeezed juices and fresh fruit and ice.

GINGER LIMEADE

SERVES 6

1$^1/_2$ cups ginger syrup (page 29)
2$^1/_2$ cups freshly squeezed lime juice
Ginger ale
1 lime, cut into wedges, for garnish

In a pitcher, combine the ginger syrup and lime juice, and mix well. Fill 6 tall 12-ounce glasses with ice. Distribute the ginger-lime mixture among the glasses. Fill the rest of each glass with ginger ale, and stir. Garnish with lime wedges.

GREEN TEA COOLER

SERVES 6

4 tea bags green tea
$^1/_2$ cup mint leaves
Zest of 1 lemon
1 quart very hot water
Sliced candied ginger, for garnish
Lemon slices, for garnish

Place the tea bags, mint, and lemon zest in a heatproof pitcher. Add the hot water and let steep for 10 minutes. Strain. Refrigerate the tea mixture for at least 2 hours to chill. Fill 6 tall 12-ounce glasses with ice. Pour the chilled tea over the ice, and garnish with candied ginger and lemon slices.

SPICED HOT APPLE PIE
SERVES 6

1 quart apple cider
$^{1}/_{2}$ vanilla bean, split in half lengthwise
2 cinnamon sticks
1 star anise
$^{1}/_{2}$ cup heavy whipping cream, whipped
Freshly grated nutmeg, for garnish

Combine the apple cider, vanilla bean, cinnamon sticks, and star anise in a saucepan over high heat. Heat until warm, but not boiling. Ladle the hot cider into 6 mugs, taking care to leave the spices in the saucepan. Top with a dollop of whipped cream, and sprinkle with nutmeg.

PASSION FRUIT FIZZLE
SERVES 6

6 passion fruit, halved, pulp removed, and
    strained (about 1$^{1}/_{2}$ cups)
$^{3}/_{4}$ cup freshly squeezed lemon juice
2 cups simple syrup (page 29)
Club soda
1 lemon, cut into wedges, for garnish

In a pitcher, combine the passion fruit purée, lemon juice, and simple syrup, and mix well. Fill 6 tall 12-ounce glasses with ice. Distribute the passion fruit mixture among the glasses. Fill the glasses with club soda, and stir. Garnish with lemon wedges.

THE BISTRO MANGO
SERVES 6

6 cups mango purée, strained
1 cup simple syrup (page 29), or more to taste
$^{1}/_{2}$ cup freshly squeezed lime juice
$^{1}/_{4}$ cup julienned fresh mint leaves
1 lime, cut into wedges, for garnish

In a pitcher, combine the mango purée, simple syrup, lime juice, and mint, and mix well. Fill 6 tall 12-ounce glasses with ice. Pour the mango mixture over the ice. Garnish with lime wedges.

BISTRO STEAMED CLAMS with ROASTED SHALLOTS and SAFFRON

SERVES 4

Since these clams are so popular on the restaurant's menu, I decided to include them here so you can share a taste of the Bistro at your next party.

4 pounds fresh clams, rinsed

$^1/_2$ cup dry white wine

$^1/_2$ cup mirin wine

$^1/_3$ cup ouzo

Zest of 1 lemon

Juice of $^1/_2$ lemon

$^1/_2$ teaspoon saffron threads

6 shallots, roasted (page 185) and coarsely chopped

2 cloves garlic, minced

$^1/_4$ cup unsalted butter

Salt

Freshly cracked black pepper

2 cups cooked basmati rice (page 189), as an
    accompaniment

In a large stockpot over high heat, combine the clams, wine, mirin, ouzo, lemon zest and juice, saffron, roasted shallots, and garlic. Bring the mixture to a boil and cook until the clams just begin to open, 3 to 4 minutes. Add the butter and continue cooking until the clams have opened completely, about 4 minutes longer. Discard any unopened clams. Season to taste with salt and pepper. Serve the clams and cooking liquid warm in large pasta bowls.

Wine Suggestion: A fruity, vibrant dry Riesling has all the fruit but not the sweetness of a Riesling. It melds wonderfully with the clams, while its crisp flavors won't compete with the complexity of the Asian sauce.

GRILLED HONEY-LEMON CHICKEN

SERVES 4

As soon as even the thought of summer is in the air, John and I start grilling. This chicken is ideal for entertaining—you can marinate the chicken earlier in the day and simply put it on the grill when guests arrive. If you're really in a pinch for time, partially cook the chicken in the oven up to two hours ahead, refrigerate, and then finish it off on the grill.

Honey-Lemon Marinade

1 shallot, chopped

2 cloves garlic, chopped

Grated zest and juice of 1 lemon

1 tablespoon honey

1 teaspoon sweet soy sauce (optional)

¹/₄ cup extra virgin olive oil

2 teaspoons chopped fresh thyme

2 teaspoons chopped fresh rosemary

1 teaspoon cracked black pepper

1 (3- to 4-pound) chicken, cut into pieces

Salt

To marinate the chicken: In a small bowl, whisk together the shallot, garlic, lemon zest and juice, honey, soy sauce, and olive oil. Add the herbs and pepper, and whisk well. Place the chicken pieces in a large bowl and pour the marinade over the top. Cover the bowl with plastic wrap, refrigerate, and marinate for at least 1 hour, or up to 6 hours.

To grill the chicken: Oil the grill. If using a charcoal grill, place the charcoal on one side of the barbecue, and light; if using a gas grill, turn on only one element and heat until very hot (to test, you should be able to hold your hand over the grill for no more than 5 seconds). Season the chicken with salt and place it on the unlit side of the grill. Cover and cook about 10 minutes. Place the chicken over the hot coals or element and cook until it reaches an internal temperature of 150°, 3 to 4 minutes. Serve hot.

Wine Suggestion: The combination of honey, lemon, and the flavor of the grill lends itself to a full-bodied Pinot Noir; try a reserve for a bit more intensity.

PORK TENDERLOIN with SPICY GLAZE AND MANGO JAM

SERVES 6

Since the tenderloin doesn't have a lot of fat in it, avoid overcooking it by roasting it quickly and just until it reaches medium doneness. Except for the cooking of the pork tenderloin, everything in this dish can be prepared in advance. The glaze can be made up to two weeks ahead of time and used on anything from grilled tuna or chicken to a stir-fry. The mango jam is delicious on a green salad topped with fresh crab—it will keep, refrigerated, for up to a week.

Mango Jam

1 tablespoon vegetable oil

1 yellow onion, diced

2 teaspoons peeled, chopped fresh ginger

1 clove garlic, chopped

1 cup mirin wine, or 1 cup dry white wine mixed with
$^1/_4$ cup honey

2 mangoes, peeled and diced

Pinch of dried red chile flakes

1 teaspoon grated lime zest

1 tablespoon lime juice

Soy sauce

Spicy Glaze

2 cloves garlic, chopped

1 tablespoon peeled, chopped fresh ginger

$^1/_2$ cup dry white wine

$^1/_4$ cup honey

$^1/_3$ cup tomato purée

$^1/_4$ cup hoisin sauce

2 teaspoons chopped fresh basil

1 teaspoon chopped fresh cilantro

2 teaspoons chile paste

Soy sauce

$2^1/_2$ pounds pork tenderloin, fat and silver skin removed

Salt

Freshly ground black pepper

1 tablespoon vegetable oil

To prepare the mango jam: Heat the vegetable oil in a large sauté pan over high heat until hot. Add the onion and cook without stirring until browned, about 5 minutes. Stir and cook without stirring 5 minutes longer. Continue this cooking process until the onions are golden brown and caramelized, 15 to 20 minutes total. Add the ginger and garlic, and sauté for about 2 minutes. Add the mirin and reduce until about $1/4$ cup remains, about 4 minutes. Let cool until tepid. Place the onion mixture, mangoes, chile flakes, and lime zest and juice in a blender, and blend until smooth. Season with soy sauce to taste and blend again. Set aside or refrigerate until ready to serve.

To prepare the glaze: Combine the garlic, ginger, and wine in a saucepan over high heat and reduce until about $1/4$ cup remains, 4 to 5 minutes. Add the honey, tomato purée, hoisin sauce, basil, and cilantro, and cook over medium heat, stirring often, until very thick, about 5 minutes. Stir in the chile paste and season with soy sauce. Set aside.

To prepare the pork tenderloin: Preheat the oven to 300°. Season the pork with salt and black pepper. Heat the oil in a large, oven-proof sauté pan over high heat until smoking hot. Add the pork and sear on all sides, about 5 minutes. Set aside about $1/2$ cup of the glaze, and brush the remaining glaze over the pork. Place the pan in the oven and roast the pork for 10 to 15 minutes, or until it reaches an internal temperature of 145° for medium doneness. Remove the pork from the oven and brush with the reserved glaze. Let it sit about 2 minutes before slicing. Slice on the diagonal against the grain.

To serve: Place the pork slices on a platter or individual plates and drizzle with mango jam. Serve hot.

Wine Suggestion: A Côtes-du-Rhône makes a good match with this dish. The blend of grapes adds depth and complexity to the wine, helping it showcase the bright Asian flavors in this dish.

3/2/03 - EXCELLENT!

ROASTED PORK LOIN with ROSEMARY-BALSAMIC GLAZE

SERVES 6

Even on relaxed Sundays John and I often have a handful of friends over for dinner. This dish, with its delicious aroma of rosemary and roasting pork, brings everyone flooding into the kitchen to reminisce and enjoy the leisurely evening.

Rosemary-Balsamic Glaze
2 cloves garlic, chopped
2 teaspoons chopped fresh rosemary
$1/4$ cup brown sugar
$3/4$ cup balsamic vinegar

3-pound boneless pork loin
Salt
Freshly ground black pepper
1 tablespoon extra virgin olive oil

Roasted Shallot Shmear (page 185), as an accompaniment

To prepare the glaze: Combine the garlic, rosemary, brown sugar, and balsamic vinegar in a saucepan over high heat, and bring just to a boil. Turn the heat to low and cook 5 minutes longer, until the brown sugar has dissolved. Set aside.

To prepare the pork loin: Preheat the oven to 300°. Season the pork loin well with salt and pepper. Heat the olive oil in a very large ovenproof sauté pan over high heat until smoking hot. Add the pork and sear well, about 5 minutes per side. Brush the pork liberally with the glaze, and set the pan in the oven. Roast the pork loin for 15 minutes, brush with more glaze, and continue roasting 15 to 20 minutes longer, or until it reaches an internal temperature of 145°, for medium doneness. Let sit about 3 minutes before slicing. Slice very thin.

To serve: Place the pork loin slices on a serving platter. Serve hot with the shmear on the side.

Wine Suggestion: A great Barbera will have deep currant notes and a slight smokiness that blend well with the balsamic glaze.

COCONUT-SHRIMP STEW

SERVES 6

John has made this stew since we were first married. The flavors are so exotic that, even after all these years, it's still one of my favorite dinners. It's a good dish to make when we're entertaining unexpectedly because it comes together quickly, yet makes an impression every time.

Coconut Broth

4 cups chicken stock (page 187)

2 (12-ounce) cans coconut milk

3 cloves garlic, chopped

1 tablespoon peeled, chopped fresh ginger

1 stalk lemongrass, coarsely chopped

Grated zest of 1 lime

1 tablespoon brown sugar or cane sugar

1 teaspoon chile paste

1 tablespoon vegetable oil

2 cloves garlic, chopped

1 red onion, julienned

2 cups julienned fresh shiitake mushrooms

1 red bell pepper, seeded and julienned

$^1/_2$ pound snow peas, ends trimmed

1 tablespoon chopped fresh basil

1 teaspoon chopped fresh cilantro

$^1/_2$ pound rice noodles, softened in hot water

2 pounds shrimp (16 to 20 count), peeled and deveined

Soy sauce

Chile paste

$^1/_2$ cup fried shallots (page 185), for garnish

To prepare the broth: Combine all the ingredients in a large stockpot over low heat and simmer until very flavorful, about 1 hour. Strain the broth through a fine sieve and set aside. (The broth can be made in advance and kept refrigerated for up to 1 week, or frozen for up to 6 months.)

To prepare the stew: Heat the vegetable oil in a large stockpot over high heat until very hot. Add the garlic and onion, and sauté for 2 minutes. Add the mushrooms, peppers, and snow peas, and sauté for 3 minutes. Add the broth and bring to a boil. Stir in the basil, cilantro, and rice noodles, and simmer until the vegetables are tender, about 5 minutes. Add the shrimp and cook just until the shrimp starts to turn pink, about 4 minutes. Remove the pan from the heat. Season the stew with soy sauce and chile paste to taste. Serve warm, garnished with fried shallots.

Wine Suggestion: I like to pour a dry Riesling with this stew. It has great backbone and doesn't bow down to the lively flavors of this dish.

vegetarian
entrées

Savory Pumpkin Cannelloni with

Sage Cream Sauce / 122

Risotto with Oven-Roasted Tomatoes / 124

Eggplant Lasagne / 125

Savory Sundried Tomato Waffles with

Mushroom Stew /126

Vegetable Fritters with

Tomato-Saffron Coulis /128

Potato Napoleons / 130

Sweet Potato and Mushroom Soufflés / 132

Butternut Gnocchi with

Roasted Shallot Sauce / 133

Pan-Fried Basmati Rice Cakes with

Cucumber Sauce / 135

Pasta with Asparagus and Goat Cheese / 137

Baked Artichokes with Herb Stuffing / 138

Smoked Onion–Herb Flan / 140

Mushroom Soba Noodles / 142

Potato and Tomatillo Gratin with

Roasted Chiles / 143

Roasted Eggplant with

Tomatoes and Peppers / 144

Zucchini Pancakes with

Roasted Corn Relish / 146

SAVORY PUMPKIN CANNELLONI with SAGE CREAM SAUCE

Even though pumpkin is a fairly starchy vegetable, this filling is light and delicate, and slightly sweet. The cannelloni are perfect for serving to a large group, because you can make them and top them with the sauce up to 24 hours in advance and refrigerate until you're ready to bake them. Then your only concern is tossing a salad and slicing a loaf of flavorful bread.

Sage Cream Sauce

3 cloves garlic, chopped

2 shallots, chopped

1 cup dry white wine

2 cups roasted vegetable stock (page 188)

1 cup heavy whipping cream

$^1/_2$ cup mascarpone (page 190)

1 teaspoon Dijon mustard

1 tablespoon chopped fresh sage

Salt

Freshly ground black pepper

Pumpkin Filling

1 tablespoon extra virgin olive oil

2 cloves garlic, chopped

1 onion, diced

$^1/_2$ cup dry sherry

4 cups pumpkin purée

$^3/_4$ cup mascarpone (page 190)

$^1/_2$ cup toasted bread crumbs (page 185)

$^3/_4$ cup freshly grated Parmesan cheese

$^3/_4$ cup grated fontina cheese

Salt

Freshly ground black pepper

1 pound fresh pasta sheets (about four 12 by 8-inch sheets)

Sage sprigs

To prepare the sauce: In a saucepan over high heat, combine the garlic, shallots, and wine. Bring the mixture to a boil and reduce until about $1/4$ cup of wine remains, about 5 minutes. Add the stock and reduce until about 1 cup of liquid remains, about 10 minutes. Add the cream, lower the heat to medium, and cook for 5 minutes. Stir in the mascarpone, mustard, and sage, and simmer until thick and the flavors are well blended, about 10 minutes. Season to taste with salt and pepper. Keep warm.

To prepare the filling: Heat the olive oil in a sauté pan over high heat until very hot. Add the garlic and onion, and sauté for 2 minutes. Add the sherry and reduce until about $1/4$ cup of liquid remains, about 4 minutes. Let cool completely. In a large bowl, combine the pumpkin, mascarpone, bread crumbs, $1/2$ cup of the Parmesan, and $1/2$ cup of the fontina, and mix well. Add the onion mixture and mix well. Season to taste with salt and pepper.

To make the cannelloni: Preheat the oven to 350°. Cut each sheet of pasta into 4 rectangles, and place about $1/3$ cup of the filling in the center of each. Roll them up and place in a 9 by 13-inch baking dish. Pour the sauce over the cannelloni and sprinkle with the remaining Parmesan and fontina cheeses. Bake until golden brown, about 30 minutes. Let sit for 5 minutes before serving. Serve warm, garnished with sage sprigs.

Wine Suggestion: A Barbera's ripe fruit flavors and smoky overtones are the perfect tribute to the simple, elegant flavors in the cannelloni.

RISOTTO with OVEN-ROASTED TOMATOES

Don't let the roasted tomatoes in this risotto scare you into thinking that the dish takes too long to prepare. The tomatoes can be roasted up to a week ahead, and they take a minimal amount of fuss and preparation. You will want to prepare the risotto just before serving, but you can always recruit a guest to give you a hand with the stirring.

6 vine-ripened tomatoes

6 small cloves garlic

¼ cup extra virgin olive oil

2 shallots, chopped

2 cups arborio rice

6 cups roasted vegetable stock (page 188),
   kept at a simmer

1 tablespoon chopped fresh basil

¾ cup grated Asiago cheese

Salt

Freshly ground black pepper

To roast the tomatoes: Preheat the oven to 425°. Place the tomatoes and garlic in a small baking dish or ovenproof sauté pan, and drizzle with about 3 tablespoons of the olive oil. Bake until the tomatoes are very brown and the skins are blistered, about 40 minutes. Let cool for about 10 minutes. Coarsely chop the tomatoes, reserving them with all the cooking liquid and garlic. Set aside. (The tomatoes can be prepared in advance and kept refrigerated for up to 1 week.)

To prepare the risotto: Heat the remaining 1 tablespoon olive oil in a large saucepan over high heat until very hot. Add the shallots and sauté for 2 minutes. Add the rice and sauté for about 2 minutes, or until the grains begin to turn opaque. Add enough hot stock to just cover the rice, about 2 cups, and cook, stirring constantly, until the stock has been absorbed. Add another 1 cup of stock and continue cooking, stirring constantly, until the stock has been absorbed. Continue until all of the stock has been absorbed but the rice is still firm. Add the reserved tomatoes, cooking liquid, and garlic, and cook, stirring continuously, until the rice is al dente. Mix in about ½ cup of the cheese, and season to taste with salt and pepper.

To serve: Serve hot in individual pasta bowls, with the remaining cheese sprinkled on top.

Wine Suggestion: The mellowed fruit of an aged Chianti goes hand in hand with the sweet, mellow roasted tomatoes.

EGGPLANT LASAGNE

I know this recipe looks complicated and time-consuming, but have no fear—you can prepare it up to two days ahead and bake it just before serving for an instant dinner party.

3 very large eggplants, cut lengthwise into
    $^1/_4$-inch-thick slices
Salt
2 tablespoons extra virgin olive oil
3 cloves garlic, chopped
1 cup loosely packed fresh basil leaves
1 tablespoon chopped fresh oregano
6 cups ricotta cheese
1 cup toasted pine nuts (page 186)
Salt
Freshly ground black pepper
1 bunch spinach, rinsed and spun dry
$1^1/_2$ cups grated fontina cheese
$^3/_4$ cup freshly grated Parmesan cheese

To prepare the eggplant: Salt the eggplant slices well and let sit for 10 minutes. Heat about 1 tablespoon of the olive oil in a very large nonstick sauté pan over high heat until smoking hot. Add as many slices of the eggplant as will fit comfortably in the pan, and sear well, about 4 minutes per side. Drain on paper towels. Continue with the remaining slices of eggplant, adding more olive oil as needed. Set aside.

To prepare the filling: Combine the garlic, basil, and oregano in the bowl of a food processor and purée. Add the ricotta cheese and pine nuts, and pulse just to mix. Transfer the mixture to a bowl, season to taste with salt and pepper, and set aside.

To assemble the lasagne: Preheat the oven to 350°. Line the bottom of a lightly oiled 9 by 13-inch baking pan with enough eggplant slices to cover. Spread one-third of the filling over the eggplant, and top with one-third of the spinach. Sprinkle with one-third of the fontina and Parmesan. Repeat twice more with the remaining ingredients. Bake the lasagne until golden brown, about 30 minutes. Remove the lasagne from the oven and let stand about 10 minutes before cutting. Serve hot.

Wine Suggestion: The cheese and eggplant in the lasagne really stand up nicely to the rough edges of a Chianti Classico.

SAVORY SUNDRIED TOMATO WAFFLES with MUSHROOM STEW

SERVES 6

I created this recipe when pressed to dazzle my vegetarian friends, who tire of the same pasta primavera when they are invited to dinner. These waffles are the perfect vehicle for the hearty mushroom stew. You can prepare the stew ahead of time, then bring it to a simmer while you cook the waffles.

Mushroom Stew

2 teaspoons extra virgin olive oil

1 onion, diced

3 cloves garlic, chopped

1 cup dry red wine

6 cups sliced wild mushrooms, such as chanterelles, morels, and porcini

2 cups roasted vegetable stock (page 188)

$^1/_2$ cup chopped pitted cured black olives

2 teaspoons chopped fresh oregano

1 teaspoon chopped fresh thyme

2 tablespoons unsalted butter

Salt

Freshly ground black pepper

Sundried Tomato Waffles

2 cups flour

$^1/_4$ teaspoon baking soda

$^1/_2$ teaspoon salt

$^1/_3$ cup minced dry-packed sundried tomatoes

2 cloves garlic, minced

2 tablespoons chopped fresh basil

$1^3/_4$ cups milk

$^1/_4$ cup club soda

4 large eggs, separated

$^1/_4$ cup unsalted butter, melted

4 ounces soft, mild goat cheese

Basil sprigs, for garnish

To prepare the stew: Heat the olive oil in a large sauté pan over high heat until very hot. Add the onion and garlic, and sauté for 2 minutes. Add the red wine and cook until reduced and the mixture is almost dry, about 4 minutes. Add the mushrooms and stock, lower the heat to medium, and cook until the mushrooms are tender, 10 to 12 minutes. Add the olives, oregano, and thyme, and cook 5 minutes longer. Stir in the butter and season to taste with salt and pepper. Keep warm. (The stew can be prepared in advance and kept refrigerated for up to 2 days. Reheat just before serving).

To prepare the waffles: Preheat the waffle iron. In a mixing bowl, combine the flour, baking soda, salt, sundried tomatoes, garlic, and basil, and mix well. In another bowl, whisk together the milk, club soda, egg yolks, and butter until smooth. Add the milk mixture into the flour mixture, and whisk until smooth. In the bowl of a heavy-duty mixer, whip the egg whites on high speed until soft peaks form. Gently fold the whites into the batter. Pour the batter into the waffle iron, and cook until golden brown. Keep warm. Repeat with remaining batter. Serve the waffles hot, topped with the stew and garnished with crumbled goat cheese and basil sprigs.

Wine Suggestion: The lush berry quality of a Merlot sets the stage for the intense, earthy flavors of the stew and the tangy contrast of the sundried tomatoes.

VEGETABLE FRITTERS with TOMATO-SAFFRON COULIS

I love to go to our local farmer's market in the summer, and the beautiful produce I found during one of my market trips inspired this dish. Use your own local market or your garden to inspire seasonal changes in the recipe.

Tomato-Saffron Coulis

3 large vine-ripened tomatoes, puréed and strained

$1/4$ cup balsamic vinegar

2 teaspoons tomato paste

2 tablespoons chopped fresh basil

$1/2$ cup extra virgin olive oil

$1/2$ teaspoon saffron threads

Salt

Freshly ground black pepper

Vegetable Fritters

3 tablespoons extra virgin olive oil

2 cloves garlic, chopped

1 small onion, minced

2 zucchini, finely grated

1 yellow squash, finely grated

1 red bell pepper, roasted, peeled, seeded, and diced (page 186)

1 large Yukon Gold potato, peeled, blanched, and grated (page 188)

$1/2$ cup whole-milk ricotta cheese

1 egg, lightly beaten

$1/2$ cup flour

1 teaspoon chopped fresh thyme

1 teaspoon chopped fresh marjoram

1 teaspoon chopped fresh basil

Salt

Freshly ground black pepper

$1/3$ cup freshly grated Parmesan cheese

Basil sprigs, for garnish

To prepare the coulis: In a bowl, whisk together the tomato purée, vinegar, tomato paste, and basil. While whisking, slowly add the olive oil and whisk until thick and emulsified. Whisk in the saffron and season to taste with salt and pepper.

To prepare the fritters: Heat 2 teaspoons of the olive oil in a large sauté pan until hot. Add the garlic and onion, and sauté until the onion is tender, about 5 minutes. Let cool for 10 minutes. In a large bowl, combine the zucchini, yellow squash, bell pepper, and potato, and mix well. Add the onion mixture, ricotta, egg, and flour, and mix well. Add the thyme, marjoram, and basil, and mix well. Season with salt and pepper.

Heat about 1 tablespoon of the olive oil in a large sauté pan over high heat until very hot. Using $1/4$ cup of batter for each fritter, pour as many fritters as will fit in the pan without overcrowding and fry until golden brown, 3 to 4 minutes per side. Keep warm. Continue with the remaining batter, adding more olive oil as needed. To serve, place the fritters on a large platter, drizzle with some of the coulis, sprinkle with the Parmesan cheese, and garnish with the basil sprigs. Serve warm, with the extra coulis on the side.

Wine Suggestion: The variety of flavors and textures of the vegetables in this dish call for a good, all-purpose, medium-bodied Pinot Noir.

POTATO NAPOLEONS

SERVES 6

I designed this recipe when I wanted to serve something a bit more sophisticated and special to some vegetarian friends. The layered effect of this potato dish is very striking. I think it looks best when served on oversized white plates with chopped fresh flat-leaf parsley sprinkled around the edges.

5 large russet potatoes, cut lengthwise into twelve
    ¹/₄-inch-thick slices

Salt

Freshly ground black pepper

3 tablespoons extra virgin olive oil

1 small yellow or sweet onion, julienned

2 cloves garlic, chopped

1 cup red wine

4 red bell peppers, roasted, peeled, seeded,
    and julienned (page 186)

1 tablespoon chopped fresh basil

1 cup grated fontina cheese

¹/₂ cup grated Asiago cheese

1 bunch watercress, rinsed and spun dry

6 tablespoons chopped fresh flat-leaf parsley,
    for garnish

To prepare the potatoes: Preheat the oven to 425°. Place the potato slices in a single layer on a well-oiled baking sheet, and bake until golden brown and tender. Season well with salt and pepper. Let cool.

To prepare the pepper mixture: Heat 1 tablespoon of the olive oil in a large sauté pan over high heat until very hot. Add the onion and garlic and sauté until the onion is tender, about 3 minutes. Add the red wine and cook until the liquid has reduced and the mixture is almost dry, 6 to 8 minutes. Add the peppers and basil and toss well. Season to taste with salt and pepper. Set aside.

To assemble the napoleons: Place 6 of the cooked potato slices in a single layer on a baking sheet. Distribute one-half of the pepper mixture over the potato slices. Top with one-half of the fontina and 6 more potato slices. Layer on the remaining pepper mixture and fontina, and top with all of the Asiago. Bake until hot and the cheese has melted, 20 to 25 minutes.

To serve: Place each napoleon on an individual plate, top with a handful of watercress, and drizzle with some of the remaining 2 tablespoons olive oil. Garnish with about 1 tablespoon of the parsley. Serve hot.

Wine Suggestion: Barbaresco has a full and spicy flavor and can be a very elegant wine. The beautiful flavors will elevate this dish even further.

When to Call for Help:

TIMES A CATERER CAN LEND A HAND

Hosting a party provides you with an opportunity to let loose with your creativity. You can have a lot of fun orchestrating and working out all of the details, from designing decorations and table settings to planning the menu and cooking. But everyone can get overwhelmed from time to time—because of time constraints, kitchen space issues, or the sheer size of the guest list—and would indeed welcome a little bit of help. Without paying to have a party fully catered, and without losing your personal touch, you can have a caterer come to the rescue in many ways and help you pull off your party flawlessly.

A caterer can:

• **Provide service staff. Be sure to clarify how servers are paid, asking if wages are hourly or if there is a flat fee, and if a gratuity is included.**

• **Prepare one or all of the more time-consuming courses, especially if your party is very large or elaborate. Even the most organized person might not have the time (or energy) to whip up a selection of appetizers or an impressive dessert for 50 people.**

• **Provide kitchen help. You can have the dinner planned and prepped, while professional cooks handle the final preparations and plating—allowing you to play host and actually sit down with your guests.**

• **Provide a trained, licensed bartender. For a very large group, this person will be able to serve a wide variety of drinks efficiently and help your guests enjoy the party safely.**

• **Provide staff to set up and clean up, from the basic table and chair setup and teardown to the more detail-oriented concerns of setting tables, helping with food presentation, and returning your house to its pre-party state.**

SWEET POTATO and MUSHROOM SOUFFLÉS

The bright orange sweet potato mixture tinged with a golden brown caramelized crust makes for a very enticing presentation, but the flavor of these soufflés will elicit just as many oohs and aahs from your guests.

$^1/_2$ **cup unsalted butter, softened**

1 tablespoon extra virgin olive oil

5 cups sliced mushrooms, such as portobellos or chanterelles

3 cloves garlic, chopped

$^1/_2$ **cup dry sherry**

$^1/_2$ **cup red wine**

Salt

Freshly ground black pepper

$3^1/_2$ **cups cooked mashed sweet potatoes**

2 tablespoons brown sugar

$^1/_2$ **cup heavy whipping cream**

3 eggs, separated

1 tablespoon chopped fresh thyme

Preheat the oven to 350°. Using 1 tablespoon of the butter, butter eight 8-ounce ramekins; set aside. Heat the olive oil in a very large sauté pan over high heat until very hot. Add the mushrooms and sauté until tender, about 4 minutes. Add the garlic and sauté for 1 minute. Add the sherry and red wine and cook until the liquid is reduced and the mixture is almost dry, 4 to 5 minutes. Add the remaining 7 tablespoons of butter, combine, and season to taste with salt and pepper. Let cool.

Place the mashed sweet potatoes in a large bowl, add the brown sugar and cream, and mix well. Add the egg yolks and thyme, and mix well. Season with salt and pepper. In the bowl of a heavy-duty mixer, whip the egg whites at high speed until they hold soft peaks. Gently fold the egg whites into the sweet potato mixture.

Divide the mushroom mixture among the ramekins. Top with the sweet potato mixture. Bake until a knife inserted in the soufflés comes out clean, about 30 minutes. Serve warm.

Wine Suggestion: The combination of the sweetness of the potatoes and the rich, earthy flavor of the mushrooms is a perfect foil for the smooth fruit of a good Merlot.

BUTTERNUT GNOCCHI with ROASTED SHALLOT SAUCE

SERVES 4

Gnocchi are fun to make, but they do take time. Prepare this dish on a leisurely Saturday afternoon, when you have extra time to spend in the kitchen. Make the dough and form the gnocchi several hours in advance, then refrigerate and cook just before serving. The shallot sauce will keep, refrigerated, for several days.

Roasted Shallot Sauce

1 dozen shallots, peeled and halved

6 cloves garlic

3/4 cup extra virgin olive oil

Grated zest and juice of 1 lemon

2 teaspoons chopped fresh marjoram

1 tablespoon balsamic vinegar

Butternut Gnocchi

1 butternut squash, split in half and seeds removed

1 tablespoon extra virgin olive oil

1/2 teaspoon ground nutmeg

2 eggs

1 cup flour

1 teaspoon kosher salt

1/4 teaspoon cracked black pepper

Salt

Freshly ground black pepper

1 cup grated Asiago cheese

continued

To prepare the sauce: Preheat the oven to 300°. Place the shallots and garlic in a roasting pan, drizzle with the olive oil, and roast until the shallots are tender, 45 minutes to 1 hour. Remove the shallots and garlic from the olive oil, reserving the oil, and coarsely chop. In a bowl, whisk together the shallots, reserved olive oil, lemon zest and juice, marjoram, and vinegar until smooth. Set aside.

To prepare the gnocchi: Increase the oven temperature to 425°. Place the butternut squash on a baking sheet, drizzle with the olive oil, and bake until tender, 40 to 50 minutes. Scrape the squash into a food processor and purée until smooth; transfer to a bowl.

Add the nutmeg and eggs to the squash purée, and mix well. Add the flour and mix just until the dough comes together. Season to taste with salt and pepper and mix well. Place the dough on a floured board and, using your hands, roll the dough out into a rope $\frac{1}{2}$ inch in diameter. Cut the dough into 1-inch pieces to form the gnocchi.

To cook the gnocchi: In a large stockpot over high heat, bring 8 cups of salted water to a rolling boil. Add about one-half of the gnocchi and cook until they float to the top. Lift out with a slotted spoon and transfer to a strainer. Repeat with the remaining gnocchi. Set aside.

In a large sauté pan over medium-high heat, bring the sauce to a boil. Add the gnocchi and heat just until warm. Season to taste with salt and pepper and toss well.

To serve: Place the gnocchi on a large platter and top with the grated Asiago cheese.

Wine Suggestion: The slight sweetness of the butternut squash makes a nice match with the mellowness of a reserve Chianti.

PAN-FRIED BASMATI RICE CAKES with CUCUMBER SAUCE

SERVES 6

The nutty flavor of basmati rice is a nice complement to the exotic spices in this dish, while the cucumber sauce adds a cool, refreshing touch. Each element of this dish can be prepared up to a day in advance, so all you'll have to do before serving is cook and garnish the rice cakes.

Cucumber Sauce

1 cup peeled, seeded, grated cucumber

2 cloves garlic, chopped

1 cup plain yogurt

1 teaspoon chopped fresh flat-leaf parsley

2 teaspoons chopped fresh mint

Salt

Freshly ground black pepper

Basmati Rice Cakes

6 cups cooked basmati rice (page 189)

2 cloves garlic, chopped

2 teaspoons peeled, chopped fresh ginger

1 small red onion, minced

2 red bell peppers, roasted, peeled, seeded, and diced (page 186)

$^3/_4$ cup heavy whipping cream

1 egg, lightly beaten

1 teaspoon ground coriander

2 teaspoons ground cumin

1 teaspoon paprika

$^1/_2$ teaspoon cayenne pepper

$^1/_2$ teaspoon ground turmeric

$^1/_2$ teaspoon ground cinnamon

Salt

Freshly ground black pepper

2 cups fresh bread crumbs

$^1/_4$ cup extra virgin olive oil

Mint sprigs, for garnish

continued

To prepare the sauce: In a bowl, combine the cucumber, garlic, and yogurt, and mix well. Add the parsley and mint, and mix well. Season to taste with salt and pepper. Set aside. (The sauce can be made in advance and kept refrigerated for up to 1 week.)

To prepare the rice cakes: In a large bowl, combine the rice, garlic, ginger, onion, red peppers, cream, and egg, and mix well. In a small bowl, combine the coriander, cumin, paprika, cayenne pepper, turmeric, and cinnamon, and mix well. Heat a small sauté pan over high heat until hot. Add the spices and dry sauté until fragrant, about 2 minutes. Add the spices to the rice mixture and mix well. Season with salt and pepper. Form the rice mixture into about twelve 1-inch patties. (The patties can be made in advance and kept refrigerated for up to 24 hours.)

To fry the rice cakes: Dredge the rice cakes in the bread crumbs. Heat about 2 tablespoons of the olive oil in a large sauté pan over high heat until smoking hot. Add as many patties as will fit in the pan without overcrowding, and cook until golden brown, 3 to 4 minutes per side. Remove from the pan and keep warm. Continue with the remaining patties, adding more olive oil as needed.

To serve: Top the rice cakes with the cucumber sauce and garnish with mint sprigs.

Wine Suggestion: It can be hard to figure out what to serve with East Indian–spiced dishes, but the spicy flavor of a dry Gewürztraminer is a natural—after all, *gewürz* means "spice" in German.

PASTA WITH ASPARAGUS AND GOAT CHEESE

This recipe is put together a bit differently than most pasta dishes. The blanched vegetables, hot pasta, and other ingredients are just tossed together before serving. The creamy goat cheese blends with the lemon and stock, making a light, tangy sauce. This dish is ideal for entertaining: If you have everything ready, all you have to do is step into the kitchen for a moment to put the finishing touches on the dish.

³/₄ pound dry linguine

3 cloves garlic, minced

1 pound asparagus spears, blanched and shocked (page 188)

¹/₂ pound snow peas, trimmed and blanched and shocked (page 188)

1 bunch spinach, rinsed well and spun dry

Grated zest of 1 lemon

¹/₄ cup hot vegetable stock (page 188)

3 tablespoons extra virgin olive oil

2 ounces soft mild goat cheese

¹/₂ teaspoon freshly cracked black pepper

Salt

¹/₂ cup freshly grated Asiago or Parmesan cheese

In a stockpot over high heat, bring about 8 cups of salted water to a boil. Add the linguine and cook until al dente, 7 to 10 minutes. Drain well.

In a very large bowl, combine the garlic, asparagus, snow peas, spinach, lemon zest, stock, olive oil, goat cheese, and pepper. Add the drained cooked pasta and toss well. Season to taste with salt and toss.

To serve, place the pasta on a large warm serving platter or in individual pasta bowls, and top with the grated cheese.

Wine Suggestion: The grassy and herbal notes of a Sauvignon Blanc balance nicely with the asparagus and other vegetables in the pasta.

BAKED ARTICHOKES with HERB STUFFING

If you prepare these artichokes in advance, you won't be in the kitchen alone working away while everyone else relaxes with a glass of wine. The artichokes can be steamed and stuffed ahead of time and left to be baked at the last moment.

6 artichokes, stems and leaves trimmed

Herb Stuffing

1 tablespoon extra virgin olive oil

1 onion, minced

2 cloves garlic, chopped

1 shallot, chopped

1 cup dry sherry

4 cups diced good-quality bread

¹/₂ cup chopped toasted hazelnuts (page 186)

1 egg, lightly beaten

1 cup roasted vegetable stock (page 188)

1 tablespoon chopped fresh basil

1 tablespoon chopped fresh thyme

1 tablespoon chopped fresh oregano

Salt

Freshly ground black pepper

¹/₂ cup freshly grated Parmesan cheese

Red Pepper Rouille (page 108), for garnish

To cook the artichokes: In a large stockpot over high heat, bring 8 cups of salted water to a boil. Add the artichokes, cover with a lid, and cook just until tender, 20 to 25 minutes. Remove the artichokes from the pot and let cool. When cool enough to handle, scoop out the center and choke of each artichoke. Set the artichokes upright in a baking dish and set aside.

To prepare the stuffing: Heat the olive oil in a large sauté pan over high heat until very hot. Add the onion, garlic, and shallot, and sauté until the onion is tender, about 5 minutes. Add the sherry and cook over high heat until the liquid has reduced and the mixture is almost dry, 6 to 8 minutes. Let cool completely. In a large bowl, combine the bread and hazelnuts. Add the onion mixture and toss well. Add the egg and stock, and mix well, adding more stock if the mixture is too dry. Add the basil, thyme, and oregano, and mix well. Season with salt and pepper.

To stuff and bake the artichokes: Preheat the oven to 350°. Fill each artichoke with stuffing and top with some of the Parmesan cheese. Bake for about 30 minutes, or until warmed through. Serve hot with Red Pepper Rouille.

Wine Suggestion: Chardonnay makes a good match with this dish. Be sure to look for one that is a Burgundian style, which has less oak and more citrus tones. If you serve these artichokes with a very oaky Chardonnay, it will be hard to taste all of the delicate flavors of the stuffing.

SMOKED ONION—HERB FLAN

We have served this flan at the Bistro for years. It's been on our menu as an appetizer, a brunch entrée, and even a lunch entrée, and it will be just as versatile for you. Try baking the crust in advance and having the rest of the ingredients prepared and waiting in the refrigerator. About an hour before you want to serve it, you'll need to take just five minutes to put the flan together before setting it in the oven to bake.

Crust

1^1/$_3$ cups flour

^{1}/$_2$ teaspoon salt

^{1}/$_4$ cup unsalted butter

^{1}/$_4$ cup shortening

6 tablespoons cold water

Smoked Onion—Herb Filling

2 tablespoons extra virgin olive oil

3 smoked onions (page 185), julienned

2 cloves garlic, chopped

^{1}/$_3$ cup freshly grated Parmesan cheese

2 teaspoons chopped fresh thyme

2 teaspoons chopped fresh marjoram

2 teaspoons chopped fresh oregano

4 ounces soft, mild goat cheese

1 cup half-and-half

4 eggs

Salt

Freshly ground black pepper

To prepare the crust: Preheat the oven to 425°. Combine the flour and salt in a bowl. Add the butter and shortening. Using your fingertips, mix until the dough resembles a coarse meal. Add the water and mix with a fork until the dough just comes together. Let rest 15 minutes.

On a well-floured board, roll the dough out into an 11-inch circle. Place in a well-greased 10-inch flan pan with a removable bottom. Bake just until the crust is set, about 10 minutes. Let cool.

To prepare the filling and assemble the flan: Heat the olive oil in a large sauté pan over high heat until very hot. Add the smoked onions and sauté until tender, about 6 minutes. Add the garlic and sauté for 1 to 2 minutes. Let cool completely.

Reduce the oven temperature to 325°. Spread the Parmesan over the bottom of the crust, and then sprinkle the herbs over it. Top with the onions, and dot with the goat cheese. In a small bowl, whisk together the half-and-half and eggs; season with salt and pepper. Pour the egg mixture over the onions and goat cheese. Bake just until the custard is set, about 30 minutes. Let cool 10 to 15 minutes before serving.

Wine Suggestion: The smokiness of the flan needs a bit of acidity as contrast. A Pinot Noir or red Burgundy will do the trick, while rounding things out with just a touch of fruit.

flan

MUSHROOM SOBA NOODLES

SERVES 6

As the drizzly weather sets in during the fall here in Portland, and our get-togethers move from the deck to the living room, I like to entertain with dinners centered around an Asian noodle dish. I'll set the coffee table with an Asian cloth, put some comfy pillows on the floor, and pull out the chopsticks and deep Asian-style bowls. The exotic setting makes slurping a steaming bowl of noodles even more enjoyable.

³/₄ **pound dried soba noodles**

1 tablespoon vegetable oil

2 cups julienned portobello mushrooms (about 4)

2 cups julienned shiitake mushrooms

1 cup julienned seasonal wild mushrooms

3 cloves garlic, chopped

1 tablespoon peeled, chopped fresh ginger

1 cup sake or dry white wine

1 cup vegetable stock (page 188)

¹/₄ **cup soy sauce**

2 tablespoons rice vinegar

1 teaspoon chopped fresh cilantro

3 green onions, white and green parts, sliced thinly on the diagonal, for garnish

In a stockpot over high heat, bring about 8 cups of water to a boil. Add the noodles and cook until al dente, 7 to 10 minutes. Drain well and set aside.

Heat the vegetable oil in a large sauté pan or wok over high heat until smoking hot. Add the mushrooms and sauté just until tender, 4 to 5 minutes. Add the garlic and ginger and sauté for 1 minute. Add the sake and cook until the liquid has reduced and the mixture is almost dry, about 4 minutes. Add the stock and cook until reduced by half, about 5 minutes. Add the soy sauce, vinegar, cilantro, and soba noodles, and toss well. Cook just until the noodles are warm, about 4 minutes. To serve, place the noodles into bowls and sprinkle with the green onions. Serve warm.

Beverage Suggestion: There's just something about a bowl brimming with noodles and a rich broth fragrant with ginger and soy that cries out for an Asian beer—without it, the picture just isn't complete. It's sort of like having spaghetti without Chianti.

POTATO and TOMATILLO GRATIN with ROASTED CHILES

SERVES 6

I prepare this gratin as an entrée, as a side dish, and even for brunch. If you want to serve it for brunch, you can cook it the night before, and then just warm it before serving the next morning.

1 onion, coarsely chopped

1 pound tomatillos, husked and rinsed

$1/4$ cup extra virgin olive oil

2 tablespoons rice vinegar

3 cloves garlic

2 teaspoons ground cumin

1 teaspoon chile powder

1 teaspoon ground coriander

1 teaspoon chopped fresh oregano

Salt

Freshly ground black pepper

6 large Yukon Gold potatoes, peeled and very thinly sliced

$1^1/2$ cups grated sharp Cheddar cheese

4 Anaheim chiles, roasted, peeled, seeded, and julienned (page 186)

$1/2$ cup sour cream

Preheat the oven to 425°. In a large, oven-proof sauté pan or baking dish, combine the onion and tomatillos, drizzle with the olive oil, and bake until the tomatillos are very soft and browned, about 40 minutes. Let cool for 15 minutes. Transfer the mixture to a blender or the bowl of a food processor, add the vinegar, garlic, cumin, chile powder, coriander, and oregano, and purée until smooth. Season to taste with salt and pepper.

Line the bottom of a well-oiled 9 by 13-inch baking pan with enough potato slices to cover. Spread one-third of the sauce over the potatoes, and top with about one-third of the cheese and one-third of the chiles. Repeat twice more with the remaining ingredients. Bake until the potatoes are very tender, about 50 minutes. Let cool for about 5 minutes before slicing. Serve warm, topped with sour cream.

Beverage Suggestion: A full-bodied, ice-cold microbrewed beer tastes just right with the chiles and sharp Cheddar.

ROASTED EGGPLANT with TOMATOES and PEPPERS

SERVES 6

To prepare this ahead of time, sear the egg-plant, top it with the pepper mixture, place it in a baking dish, and cover and refrigerate until ready to bake. When your guests arrive, finishing the dish is a breeze: Simply bake the egg-plant until tender.

3 eggplants, ends trimmed, halved lengthwise

1 tablespoon kosher salt

$^1/_4$ cup extra virgin olive oil

3 large vine-ripened tomatoes, peeled, seeded, and chopped (pages 188 and 189)

1 red onion, julienned

3 cloves garlic, chopped

3 red, yellow, or orange bell peppers, roasted, peeled, seeded, and julienned (page 186)

2 anchovies, minced (optional)

2 teaspoons chopped fresh basil

2 teaspoons chopped fresh flat-leaf parsley

Juice of $^1/_2$ lemon

Salt

Freshly ground black pepper

Preheat the oven to 375°. Sprinkle the cut sides of the eggplant with the kosher salt and let sit for about 10 minutes. Heat about 1 tablespoon of the olive oil in a large sauté pan over high heat until smoking hot. Add two of the eggplant halves, cut side down, and sear until golden brown, 4 to 5 minutes. Drain on paper towels. Remove from the pan and set aside. Continue with the remaining eggplant, adding an additional tablespoon of olive oil if necessary.

In a small bowl, combine the tomatoes, onion, garlic, peppers, anchovies, basil, parsley, and lemon juice, and toss well. Season to taste with salt and pepper. Place the eggplant halves, cut side up, in a large roasting pan and top with the tomato mixture. Drizzle with the remaining 2 tablespoons olive oil. Cover with a lid or foil and roast for about 40 minutes. Remove the lid or foil and continue roasting until the eggplant is fork-tender, about 10 minutes.

To serve, place the eggplant halves on a large platter or individual plates. Pour the cooking juices over the eggplant. Serve warm.

Wine Suggestion: When you sear and roast the eggplant, the flavors really intensify. A rich, jammy Merlot suits this dish well.

Centerpieces

Your table is as much a part of your party as you and what you serve, but that doesn't mean you need elaborate table settings and centerpieces. You can easily create beautiful centerpieces without much time, effort, or expense. I've used the following ideas over the years to enhance my table for simple and more elegant gatherings:

- Set one or three (an odd number) inexpensive potted orchids in Chinese to-go containers, and place moss on top of the soil to cover.

- Float gardenias and candles in a large beautiful bowl filled with water.

- Fill a simple ceramic or glass pitcher with daisies or lilacs.

- Set a florist's frog in a large bowl. Fill the bowl with attractive stones to cover the frog. Place three Asian lilies in the frog, and fill the bowl with water.

- Set three to five (an odd number) 4-inch pots of herbs in terra-cotta or other decorative pots, and place moss on top of the soil to cover.

- Cut long pieces of fresh ivy or other hearty trailing plant, and place them in the center of the table to make a runner. Set votive candles throughout the ivy.

- Fill a glass vase with kumquats and pomegranates, and add water to cover.

- The day before, fill three old-fashioned canning jars with a dozen nasturtium blossoms each, and add white wine vinegar to cover. Place the lids on the jars, and let sit for 24 hours. The color from the flowers will infuse into the vinegar.

- Scatter fresh rose petals down the center of the table as a runner. Place several votive candles among the petals.

- Place a candle in a short glass vase (use a candle that will fit snugly in the vase). Wrap handmade paper around the vase, leaving no overhang, and secure with raffia. Light the candle just before seating your guests.

ZUCCHINI PANCAKES with ROASTED CORN RELISH

Because of the last-minute preparation and cooking that these pancakes require, I suggest you make them for a smaller group—otherwise, you'll be standing at the stove, flipping orders like a short-order cook.

Roasted Corn Relish

3 tablespoons extra virgin olive oil

Kernels cut from 3 ears corn (about 3 cups)

3 cloves garlic, chopped

1 red onion, julienned

2 vine-ripened tomatoes, seeded (page 188), and chopped

1 teaspoon chopped fresh cilantro

2 tablespoons balsamic vinegar

Salt

Freshly cracked black pepper

Zucchini Pancakes

1 (12-ounce) can coconut milk

2 cloves garlic, minced

2 teaspoons chopped fresh basil

2 zucchini, grated

$1/3$ cup rice flour

2 egg whites

Salt

Freshly ground black pepper

2 tablespoons extra virgin olive oil

1 cup sour cream

Cilantro sprigs, for garnish

To prepare the relish: Heat 1 tablespoon of the olive oil in a large sauté pan over high heat until smoking hot. Add the corn and sear, without stirring, for 2 to 3 minutes. Toss well and sear 2 to 3 minutes longer. Add the garlic and onion and sauté for 2 minutes. Add the tomatoes and cilantro and toss well. Add the vinegar and remaining 2 tablespoons olive oil and toss again to mix. Season to taste with salt and cracked pepper. Set aside.

To prepare the pancakes: In a large bowl, combine the coconut milk, garlic, basil, and zucchini, and mix well. Slowly add the rice flour and mix well. In the bowl of a heavy-duty mixer, whip the egg whites at high speed until they hold soft peaks. Gently fold the egg whites into the batter. Season with salt and pepper.

Preheat the oven to 250°. Heat about 1 tablespoon of the olive oil in a large nonstick sauté pan over high heat until hot. Using $1/4$ cup of batter for each pancake, pour as many pancakes as will fit in the pan. Cook until the batter bubbles, about 3 minutes. Flip and cook 3 minutes longer, until golden brown. Keep warm in the oven while preparing the remaining pancakes.

To serve: Place 2 pancakes on each individual plate and top with a heaping $1/2$ cup of the relish. Spoon a dollop of sour cream on top, and garnish with a cilantro sprig. Serve warm.

Wine Suggestion: The lush fruit of a reserve Pinot Noir will marry well with the sweetness of the corn and coconut milk in this dish.

desserts

Seared Apples with Brandy-Vanilla
   Syrup / 150

Chocolate and Macadamia Nut—Filled
   Wontons with Mango-Ginger Dipping
   Sauce / 151

Brandy-Pear Tart / 152

Blackberry Crème Caramel / 154

Peach Pie with Oatmeal-Pecan Crust / 155

Dried Cherry Coffee Cake / 156

Double-Crusted Lemon-Ricotta Tart / 157

Pecan Pie with Two Chocolates and
   a Spice Crust / 158

Silky Chocolate-Raspberry Tart / 159

Mixed Berry Clafoutis / 160

Flourless Chocolate-Hazelnut Torte / 161

Passion Fruit—Lime Cheesecake / 162

Lemon-Mascarpone Tart / 163

Panna Cotta with Blackberry Compote / 164

Cherry Tart with Strawberries and
   Dark Chocolate / 166

Chocolate Volcano Birthday Cake / 167

Summer Pudding / 169

Cinnamon Pound Cakes with
   Mascarpone-Coffee Meringue / 170

Pumpkin Bread Pudding with
   Candied Pecan Topping / 172

Mango Tart with Coconut-Macadamia
   Crust / 174

Chocolate Mousse with
   Spice-Poached Pears / 175

Lemon Pancakes with
   Raspberry Compote / 176

Bourbon-Soaked Babas with
   Marinated Fruit / 178

Deep-Fried Coconut Pâte à Choux / 180

Caramelized Strawberries with
   Baked Meringue / 181

Lime-Coconut Chess Pie / 182

Rhubarb Crème Brûlée / 183

SEARED APPLES with BRANDY-VANILLA SYRUP

SERVES 6

You can prepare most of this simple yet quite elegant dessert in advance. The syrup will keep for up to two weeks if refrigerated; bring it to a boil before serving. Sear and roast the apples up to a day ahead, and then reheat in a 200° oven for about 10 minutes.

1 cup sugar

2 teaspoons ground cinnamon

1 teaspoon ground ginger

1 teaspoon ground nutmeg

1 teaspoon ground allspice

6 Granny Smith apples, peeled, cored, and halved

1 tablespoon vegetable oil

Brandy-Vanilla Syrup

1 cup water

$^1/_4$ cup brandy

1 vanilla bean, split in half lengthwise

$^3/_4$ cup sugar

1 cup crème fraîche (page 190), or 1 pint vanilla
    ice cream, as an accompaniment

To prepare the apples: Preheat the oven to 350°. In a small bowl, combine the sugar, cinnamon, ginger, nutmeg, and allspice, and mix well. Dredge the apples in the sugar, turning them to coat well. Heat the oil in a large, ovenproof sauté pan over high heat until very hot. Place the apples in the pan, cut side down, and sear well until the sugar caramelizes, 2 to 3 minutes. Place the pan in the oven and bake for about 35 minutes, or until the apples are tender.

To prepare the syrup: In a saucepan over high heat, combine the water, brandy, vanilla bean, and sugar. Bring the mixture to a boil and cook about 5 minutes, or until thick and the sugar has dissolved. Discard the vanilla bean. Keep warm.

To serve: Place two apple halves on each plate, ladle about $^1/_4$ cup of the warm syrup over the apples, and top with a dollop of crème fraîche or a scoop of vanilla ice cream. Serve warm.

CHOCOLATE and MACADAMIA NUT—FILLED WONTONS with MANGO-GINGER DIPPING SAUCE

SERVES 6

Anything in a wonton wrapper sounds good to me! Be sure to serve these warm. For a fun presentation, serve the wontons on an Asian-style platter and set out a basket of chopsticks. To save time, fill and fold the wontons in advance: Just place them in a single layer on a baking sheet, without letting their edges touch, cover with plastic wrap, and keep refrigerated for up to a day. Alternately, freeze them on a baking sheet, and then transfer to a reclosable plastic bag and keep frozen for up to 6 months.

Mango-Ginger Dipping Sauce

1 mango, peeled and diced

2 teaspoons chopped candied ginger

1/4 cup brown sugar

Juice of 1/2 lemon

Chocolate-Macadamia Filling

4 ounces bittersweet chocolate, finely chopped

1/3 cup ground toasted macadamia nuts (page 186)

2 teaspoons finely minced candied ginger

2 ounces cream cheese, softened

2 tablespoons granulated sugar

Pinch ground cinnamon

30 wonton wrappers

Vegetable oil, for deep-frying

1/2 cup confectioners' sugar, for dusting

To prepare the dipping sauce: Place the mango, ginger, brown sugar, and lemon juice in a blender, and blend until smooth. Refrigerate until ready to use. (The sauce can be made in advance and refrigerated for up to 2 days, or frozen for up to 6 months.)

To prepare the filling: Combine the chocolate, nuts, and ginger in a bowl and mix well. Add the cream cheese, granulated sugar, and cinnamon and mix well.

To assemble the wontons: Place a wonton wrapper on a work surface. Place about 1 teaspoon of the filling in the center of the wrapper. Using your fingers, lightly moisten the edges with water. Fold the sides of the wrapper over the filling to form a triangle, and gently press to seal. Bring the two corners on the longest end of the triangle together and pinch well. Repeat with the remaining wrappers and filling.

To fry and serve the wontons: Heat about 4 inches of oil in a heavy saucepan over high heat until it reaches 350°. Add about 5 wontons, or as many as will fit in the pan, and cook until golden brown, 3 to 4 minutes. Drain on paper towels and dust with confectioners' sugar. Continue with the remaining wontons. Serve warm with the dipping sauce.

BRANDY-PEAR TART

SERVES 8

Be sure to choose pears that aren't too ripe for this tart, or they'll get mushy when cooked. All of the components can be made well in advance and then put together just before baking. If you bake it ahead of time, reheat it in a 250° oven for about 15 minutes before serving.

Crust

1¹/₂ cups flour

¹/₂ cup sugar

1 teaspoon pure vanilla extract

7 tablespoons unsalted butter, diced

¹/₂ teaspoon salt

1 egg

Brandy-Pear Filling

8 pears, peeled, cored, and diced

³/₄ cup sugar

¹/₃ cup pear brandy or brandy

¹/₃ cup Riesling or other sweet white wine

2 large slices peeled fresh ginger

¹/₂ vanilla bean, split in half lengthwise

1 teaspoon ground cinnamon

1 teaspoon ground allspice

¹/₂ teaspoon ground nutmeg

2 tablespoons unsalted butter

Ground cinnamon, for dusting

1 quart vanilla ice cream, as an accompaniment

To prepare the crust: Combine the flour, sugar, vanilla, butter, and salt in the bowl of a food processor, and process until the mixture resembles a coarse meal. With the machine running, add the egg through the feed tube and process just until the dough comes together. Roll the dough into a ball, wrap tightly with plastic wrap, and refrigerate for about 20 minutes to chill. (The dough can be prepared in advance and kept refrigerated for up to 4 days, or frozen for up to 6 months.)

To prepare the filling: Toss the pears with the sugar. Combine the pears, brandy, wine, ginger, and vanilla bean in a saucepan over medium heat and cook, stirring occasionally, until the pears are tender, about 4 minutes. Remove the pears from the liquid, and set aside. Reduce the liquid over high heat until very thick, about 3 minutes. Remove the pan from the heat, and stir in the cinnamon, allspice, nutmeg, and butter. Let cool completely.

To assemble and bake the tart: Preheat the oven to 350°. Divide the dough in half. On a well-floured board, roll half of the dough out into a 10-inch circle. Press it into a well-greased 9-inch tart or flan pan with a removable bottom. Spread the cooled pears over the bottom crust, and pour the syrup over the pears. Roll the other half of the dough into a 10-inch circle. Place over the filling, and press to seal the edges. Prick the top crust with a fork. Bake until golden brown, about 40 minutes. Let cool about 15 minutes.

To serve: Serve warm with vanilla ice cream. Lightly dust the rim of each individual plate with cinnamon.

BLACKBERRY CRÈME CARAMEL

SERVES 6

This dessert is best made at least 24 hours ahead, so the caramelized sugar has a chance to transform into a smooth sauce. It's great when you need to have some of your menu prepared in advance.

1½ cups sugar
¼ cup water
¾ cup blackberry purée, strained
½ teaspoon pure vanilla extract
5 large eggs, lightly beaten
2 cups half-and-half

1 cup heavy whipping cream, whipped, for garnish
Mint sprigs, for garnish

To prepare the caramel: In a heavy saucepan over high heat, combine 1 cup of the sugar and the water and cook, without stirring, until the sugar begins to turn brown, about 10 minutes. Swirl the pan to even the color, and cook just until the sugar is golden brown. Distribute the caramelized sugar among six 8-ounce ramekins. Set aside.

To prepare the custard: In a large bowl, whisk together the blackberry purée, vanilla, eggs, and the remaining ½ cup sugar until smooth. Heat the half-and-half in a saucepan over high heat just until it comes to a boil. Whisk about 1 cup of the hot half-and-half into the egg mixture to temper. Pour the egg mixture into the remaining half-and-half, and whisk until smooth. Using a large spoon, skim the foam from the surface of the custard. Divide the custard among the ramekins. Place the ramekins in a roasting pan, and fill the pan with enough hot water to reach about halfway up the sides of the ramekins. Carefully set the pan in the oven and bake until the custard is set, about 50 minutes. Remove the ramekins from the roasting pan and refrigerate at least 4 hours.

To serve: To serve, run a knife around the edges of the ramekins and turn each one over onto a plate to release the crème caramel. Top with whipped cream and garnish with a mint sprig.

PEACH PIE with OATMEAL-PECAN CRUST

This dessert makes the ultimate ending to a Sunday night dinner in summer. The pie can be made several hours in advance and then warmed in a 200° to 250° oven just before serving. Be sure to use peaches that are ripe but not too soft. If an oatmeal crust doesn't sound appealing to you, use a traditional pâte brisée instead.

Oatmeal-Pecan Crust

2 cups flour

³/₄ cup oatmeal

¹/₄ cup ground toasted pecans (page 186)

1 cup sugar

1 egg yolk

2 teaspoons pure vanilla extract

1 cup unsalted butter, diced

Peach Filling

6 peaches, peeled (page 189) and sliced

1 cup sugar

¹/₄ cup bourbon

2 tablespoons cornstarch

2 teaspoons ground cinnamon

1 teaspoon ground ginger

2 tablespoons unsalted butter

1 quart high-quality vanilla ice cream, as an
    accompaniment

To prepare the crust: In the bowl of a food processor, combine the flour, oatmeal, pecans, and sugar. With the motor running, add the egg yolk, vanilla, and butter through the feed tube and process until a dough forms on top of the blades. (The dough can be prepared in advance. Roll it into a ball, wrap tightly with plastic wrap, and refrigerate for up to 4 days, or freeze for up to 6 months.) Cut the dough in half. On a well-floured board, roll the dough out into two 10-inch circles. Set aside.

To prepare the filling and bake the pie: Preheat the oven to 425°. Place the peaches in a bowl. Add the sugar, bourbon, cornstarch, cinnamon, and ginger, and mix well. Place one circle of dough in a 9-inch pie plate, and top with the filling. Dot with the butter. Lay the top crust over the filling and crimp the edges. Bake for 15 minutes. Lower the heat to 350° and bake 25 to 30 minutes longer, or until golden brown. Let cool for about 15 minutes. Serve warm with vanilla ice cream.

DRIED CHERRY COFFEE CAKE

Whenever John and I have a brunch at our house, it usually starts around noon. Since we're not morning people, I like to make this cake for our guests. It's easy and quick to prepare, unlike many other breakfast breads that require you to get up hours before dawn in order to have them baked in time.

Hazelnut Topping

2 cups chopped toasted, skinned hazelnuts (page 186)

$^1/_4$ cup unsalted butter, softened

$^1/_4$ cup brown sugar

$^1/_4$ cup flour

$1^1/_2$ teaspoons ground cinnamon

$^1/_2$ teaspoon ground ginger

$^1/_2$ teaspoon ground nutmeg

$^1/_2$ teaspoon ground allspice

Dried Cherry Coffee Cake

1 cup unsalted butter, softened

2 cups granulated sugar

2 eggs

1 teaspoon pure vanilla extract

2 cups flour

2 teaspoons baking powder

Pinch salt

1 cup sour cream

$1^1/_2$ cups coarsely chopped dried cherries

To prepare the topping: In a bowl, combine the nuts, butter, sugar, and flour, and mix well to form a crumbly mixture. Add the spices and mix well. Set aside.

To prepare the cake: Preheat the oven to 350°. In the bowl of a heavy-duty mixer, beat the butter and granulated sugar at high speed until creamy and a pale lemon color, about 4 minutes. Add the eggs, one at a time, beating well after each addition. Add the vanilla and mix well. In a small bowl, mix together the flour, baking powder, and salt. Add about half of the flour to the butter mixture and beat well. Add about half of the sour cream and beat well. Repeat with remaining flour and sour cream. Fold in the dried cherries.

Pour about half of the batter into a well-greased 9 by 13-inch baking pan. Cover the batter with half of the topping. Spread the remaining batter over the topping, and sprinkle with the remaining topping. Bake until golden brown and until a knife inserted in the cake comes out clean, 45 to 50 minutes. Let cool for about 10 minutes before slicing. Serve warm.

DOUBLE-CRUSTED LEMON-RICOTTA TART

SERVES 10

I like to use ricotta as a filling in tarts because it's creamy yet has a bit of texture. In this recipe, I combine ricotta with lemon and pine nuts, giving the tart a unique texture and also an uncommon flavor. The seasonal berries complement the tart and create a beautiful presentation.

Crust

3 cups flour

$1/2$ cup sugar

$3/4$ cup plus 2 tablespoons unsalted butter, diced

1 teaspoon salt

1 egg yolk

Lemon-Ricotta Filling

2 cups whole-milk ricotta cheese

1 cup sugar

2 eggs

1 cup toasted pine nuts (page 186)

Grated zest and juice of 1 lemon

$1/2$ teaspoon pure vanilla extract

1 cup heavy whipping cream, whipped, as an accompaniment

2 pints fresh seasonal berries, rinsed, as an accompaniment

Mint sprigs, for garnish

To prepare the crust: Combine the flour, sugar, butter, and salt in the bowl of a food processor, and process until the mixture resembles a coarse meal. With the motor running, add the egg yolk through the feed tube and process until a dough forms on top of the blades. Roll the dough into a ball, wrap tightly with plastic wrap, and refrigerate for 15 to 30 minutes. (The dough can be prepared in advance and kept refrigerated for up to 4 days, or frozen for up to 6 months.)

To prepare the filling: Combine the ricotta, sugar, and eggs in a bowl, and mix well. Add the pine nuts, lemon zest and juice, and vanilla, and mix well.

To assemble and bake the tart: Preheat the oven to 350°. Cut the dough in half. On a well-floured board, roll half of the dough into a 10-inch circle, and press it into a well-greased 9-inch tart or flan pan with a removable bottom. Spoon on the filling. Fold the excess dough over the filling, and brush the edge of the dough with water to moisten. Roll the other half of the dough into an 8-inch circle, place it over the filling, and press to seal the edges. Prick with a fork. Bake until golden brown, about 40 minutes. Let cool completely.

Serve with whipped cream and berries, and garnish with mint.

PECAN PIE with TWO CHOCOLATES and a SPICE CRUST

SERVES 12

The texture of this pie is wonderful. Your fork will meet chunks of white and bittersweet chocolate before it reaches the gooey bottom layer. I like to serve it warm, so that a scoop of high-quality vanilla-bean ice cream on top just starts to melt as you take your first bite. If you can't bake the pie right before serving, gently reheat it in a 200° to 250° oven, just until warm.

Spice Crust

1 1/3 cups flour

1 teaspoon ground cinnamon

1 teaspoon ground ginger

1 teaspoon ground allspice

Pinch salt

1/4 cup unsalted butter, diced

1/4 cup shortening

6 tablespoons cold water, plus additional if needed

Pecan-Chocolate Filling

2 cups ground toasted pecans (page 186)

3 ounces bittersweet chocolate, chopped

3 ounces white chocolate, chopped

3 eggs

1 cup dark corn syrup

3/4 cup brown sugar

1 teaspoon pure vanilla extract

1 pint high-quality vanilla ice cream, as an
    accompaniment

4 ounces white chocolate, shaved

4 ounces bittersweet chocolate, shaved

To prepare the crust: Preheat the oven to 425°. Combine the flour, cinnamon, ginger, allspice, and salt in a bowl. Add the butter and shortening. Using your fingertips, mix until the dough resembles a coarse meal. Add the water and mix with a fork just until the dough comes together. Let rest for at least 15 minutes. (The dough can be prepared in advance. Roll it into a ball, wrap tightly with plastic wrap, and refrigerate for up to 4 days, or freeze for up to 6 months.)

On a well-floured board, roll the dough out into a 10-inch circle. Place the dough in a 9-inch pie plate and flute the edges. Bake just until the crust is set, about 10 minutes. Let cool completely.

To prepare the filling and bake the pie: Lower the oven temperature to 350°. Spread the pecans over the bottom of the crust and top with the chocolate. In a bowl, whisk together the eggs, corn syrup, brown sugar, and vanilla until smooth. Pour the egg mixture over the pecans and chocolate. Bake until just set, 30 to 40 minutes, or until a knife inserted in the pie comes out clean.

To serve: Serve warm with vanilla ice cream, garnished with shaved white and bittersweet chocolate.

SILKY CHOCOLATE-RASPBERRY TART

SERVES 16

Serve this dessert with care, because it is very rich and intense—it will definitely push your guests over the edge and into decadence! This beautiful tart is deceptive, because it is actually quite simple to prepare.

Chocolate Tart Crust

1 cup flour

$^1/_2$ cup cocoa powder

$^1/_2$ cup sugar

1 teaspoon pure vanilla extract

7 tablespoons unsalted butter, diced

$^1/_2$ teaspoon salt

1 egg

Chocolate-Raspberry Filling

1 pint raspberries, rinsed

1$^1/_2$ cups heavy whipping cream

2 tablespoons unsalted butter

12 ounces bittersweet chocolate, coarsely chopped

$^1/_4$ cup raspberry liqueur

1 cup heavy whipping cream, whipped, as an
     accompaniment

Mint sprigs, for garnish

2 pints fresh raspberries, rinsed, for garnish

To prepare the crust: Preheat the oven to 375°. In the bowl of a food processor, combine the flour, cocoa, sugar, vanilla, butter, and salt. Pulse until the mixture resembles a fine meal. With the motor running, add the egg and process just until the dough comes together. Form the dough into a ball. (The dough can be prepared in advance. Roll it into a ball, wrap tightly with plastic wrap, and refrigerate for up to 4 days, or freeze for up to 6 months.) On a well-floured board, roll the dough out into a 12-inch circle. Press the dough into a well-greased 10-inch tart or flan pan with a removable bottom. Bake the crust until crisp, about 20 minutes. Let cool about 10 minutes.

To prepare the filling and assemble the tart: Place the raspberries in the bottom of the cooled crust. Heat the cream and butter in a saucepan over medium heat just until boiling. Meanwhile, place the chocolate in the bowl of a food processor and process until finely chopped. With the motor running, pour the hot cream through the feed tube and process until smooth. Add the raspberry liqueur and process until well blended. Pour the filling into the prepared crust and refrigerate until set, about 2 hours.

Serve chilled, topped with a dollop of whipped cream and garnished with mint sprigs and fresh raspberries.

MIXED BERRY CLAFOUTIS

SERVES 8

Clafouti, an old-fashioned dessert similar to a custard but with the addition of a small amount of flour, is traditionally made in a large baking pan. I make mine in individual ramekins, because the presentation is so much nicer. Instead of just a lump on a plate, you present a nice little dish topped with confectioners' sugar and mint. You can substitute any fruit at the peak of its season in this recipe—I especially like raspberries, blueberries, or, in the winter, poached pears.

4 cups pitted sour pie cherries

2 cups blackberries or Marionberries, rinsed

4 eggs

1¼ cups milk

¼ cup orange brandy

1 teaspoon ground cinnamon

⅓ cup flour

½ cup granulated sugar

Pinch salt

¼ cup confectioners' sugar, for dusting

Mint sprigs, for garnish

Preheat the oven to 350°. Butter eight 8-ounce ramekins. Distribute the cherries and berries among the ramekins. Set aside.

In a mixing bowl, whisk together the eggs, milk, and brandy. Add the cinnamon, flour, granulated sugar, and salt, and whisk until smooth. Pour the batter over the cherries and berries. Bake until golden brown, 35 to 40 minutes. Let cool for about 15 minutes. Dust with the confectioners' sugar. Serve warm in the ramekins.

FLOURLESS CHOCOLATE-HAZELNUT TORTE

SERVES 14

This is one of my old standbys—I pull this recipe out when I want to make something sophisticated, but in a hurry! The torte comes together very quickly, and requires only about 25 minutes of baking. And if I'm really short on time, I skip the glaze, dust the torte with confectioners' sugar, and serve it with fresh fruit.

Chocolate-Hazelnut Torte

1 pound bittersweet chocolate, chopped

1 cup unsalted butter, diced

¹/₄ cup cocoa powder

¹/₄ cup hazelnut liqueur

¹/₂ teaspoon pure vanilla extract

5 eggs

2 cups ground toasted, skinned hazelnuts (page 186)

Chocolate Glaze

1 cup heavy whipping cream

12 ounces bittersweet chocolate, chopped

1 cup heavy whipping cream, whipped, as an accompaniment

¹/₂ cup chopped toasted, skinned hazelnuts (page 186), for garnish

Mint sprigs, for garnish

To prepare the torte: Preheat the oven to 350°. In the top of a double boiler, heat the chocolate and butter until the chocolate is melted. Remove from the heat and stir. Add the cocoa powder, liqueur, vanilla, and eggs, and mix well. Add the hazelnuts and mix well. Pour the batter into a greased 9-inch cake pan lined with parchment. Bake until the cake is just barely set, 25 to 30 minutes. Let the cake cool in the pan for about 15 minutes, then remove from the pan and place on a rack. Let cool completely.

To prepare the glaze: Heat the cream in a saucepan over high heat until it just comes to a boil. Meanwhile, place the chocolate in the bowl of a food processor and process until finely chopped. With the machine running, pour the hot cream through the feed tube and process until smooth. Transfer the glaze to a bowl and let cool for 10 minutes.

To glaze the torte: Set the rack with the cooled torte over a baking sheet. Pour all of the glaze over the center of the torte, letting it run over and down the sides. (You may need to jiggle the torte to help the glaze flow over the sides.) Refrigerate for at least 2 hours, or up to 24 hours.

To serve: Let the torte stand at room temperature for at least 30 minutes. Serve with whipped cream, and garnish with chopped toasted hazelnuts and mint sprigs.

PASSION FRUIT–LIME CHEESECAKE

SERVES 12

If you're throwing a party and plan on serving several appetizers or an entrée that calls for last-minute attention, you'll want to serve a dessert that you can make far in advance. This is a perfect candidate, since it can be kept refrigerated for up to two days—and with its exotic flavors, it isn't just another run-of-the-mill cheesecake.

Cashew-Coconut Crust

1¹/₂ cups ground toasted cashews (page 186)

³/₄ cup coconut

¹/₄ cup sugar

¹/₂ teaspoon ground ginger

6 tablespoons unsalted butter, melted

Passion Fruit–Lime Filling

2 pounds cream cheese

1¹/₂ cups sugar

5 eggs

¹/₄ cup dark rum

Grated zest and juice of 1 lime

2 passion fruit, pulp removed and seeds strained

1 cup heavy whipping cream, whipped, as an
    accompaniment

Zest of 1 lime, as garnish

¹/₂ cup toasted fresh coconut, as garnish

To prepare the crust: In a bowl, combine the cashews, coconut, sugar, and ginger, and mix well. Add the butter and mix well. Press the dough into a well-greased 10-inch springform pan. Chill for 30 minutes.

To prepare the filling: Preheat the oven to 350°. In the bowl of a food processor, combine the cream cheese and sugar, and process until smooth. Scrape down the sides. With the machine running, add the eggs, one at a time, through the feed tube and process until smooth. Add the rum and process to mix. Divide the filling among 2 bowls. Add the lime zest and juice to one bowl of filling and mix well. Add the passion fruit to the other bowl of filling and mix well.

To assemble the cheesecake: Pour the lime filling into the prepared crust. Pour the passion fruit filling over the top, and then swirl with a large spoon. Bake for 50 minutes to 1 hour, or until a knife inserted in the cheesecake comes out clean. Let cool for 20 minutes, and then refrigerate for at least 2 hours.

To serve: Serve chilled, topped with whipped cream and garnished with lime zest and toasted coconut.

LEMON-MASCARPONE TART

SERVES 12

Inspired by the flavors of Provence, I wanted to create a dessert that showcased the lemon and lavender that are so prevalent in the region's cuisine. For a garnish with visual impact, cover the tart with shaved white chocolate and then top it with candied lemon zest.

Lavender-Almond Crust

1¹/₂ cups flour

¹/₂ cup ground toasted almonds (page 186)

¹/₂ cup confectioners' sugar

¹/₂ teaspoon almond extract

Pinch salt

¹/₂ teaspoon crushed dried lavender

1 cup unsalted butter, diced

Lemon-Mascarpone Filling

2¹/₂ cups mascarpone (page 190)

1 cup granulated sugar

3 eggs

Finely chopped zest and juice of 1 lemon

Dash pure vanilla extract

1 cup heavy whipping cream, whipped, as an
    accompaniment

To prepare the crust: Preheat the oven to 350°. In the bowl of a food processor, combine the flour, almonds, confectioners' sugar, almond extract, salt, and lavender, and process briefly to mix. With the machine running, add the butter, a few pieces at a time, through the feed tube, and process until a dough forms on top of the blades. (The dough can be prepared in advance. Roll it into a ball, wrap tightly with plastic wrap, and refrigerate for up to 4 days, or freeze for up to 6 months.) Press the dough into a well-greased 10-inch tart or flan pan with a removable bottom. Bake just until the crust is set, about 10 minutes. Let cool completely.

To prepare the filling and bake the tart: While the crust is cooling, combine the mascarpone, granulated sugar, and eggs in a mixing bowl, and mix well. Add the lemon zest, lemon juice, and vanilla, and mix well. Pour the filling into the cooled crust and bake 25 to 30 minutes, or until a knife inserted in the tart comes out clean. Let cool.

To serve: Serve at room temperature or chilled with whipped cream.

PANNA COTTA with BLACKBERRY COMPOTE

SERVES 8

Panna cotta, a traditional Italian dessert, is creamy, light, and simple. In this version I've included candied ginger and cinnamon to give it a more exotic flavor. I love the contrast of warm and cold in desserts, and here the warm compote really plays up the cool and silky texture of the panna cotta. Both elements of this dessert can be made at least a day before serving, which means they're great for when you have guests.

Panna Cotta

4 cups heavy whipping cream

2 teaspoons unflavored gelatin

$1/2$ cup sugar

2 cinnamon sticks

1 vanilla bean, split in half lengthwise

2 teaspoons minced candied ginger

5 egg whites

Blackberry Compote

1 tablespoon unsalted butter

2 cups blackberries, rinsed

$1/4$ cup sugar

$1/4$ cup blackberry or raspberry liqueur

$1/2$ teaspoon ground ginger

$1/2$ teaspoon ground cinnamon

1 cup heavy whipping cream, whipped, as an accompaniment

Mint sprigs, for garnish

To prepare the *panna cotta*: In a saucepan over medium heat, combine 1 cup of the cream and the gelatin, sugar, cinnamon sticks, and vanilla bean. Heat the mixture, stirring constantly, until the gelatin has dissolved, about 2 minutes. Transfer to a large bowl, and whisk in the remaining 3 cups cream. Remove and discard the cinnamon sticks. Scrape the seeds from the center of the vanilla bean into the cream mixture, and then discard the bean. Add the candied ginger, and whisk well. Let cool until tepid.

In the bowl of a heavy-duty mixer, whip the egg whites at high speed until they hold soft peaks. Gently fold the egg whites into the cream mixture. Lightly butter eight 8-ounce ramekins. Divide the mixture among the ramekins. Chill, uncovered, for at least 4 hours, or up to 24 hours.

To prepare the compote: Heat the butter in a large sauté pan over high heat until melted and bubbly. Add the berries and sauté for 2 minutes. Add the sugar and liqueur and cook until the sugar dissolves, about 2 minutes. (Be careful: The liqueur may ignite. If it does, cool the berry mixture until the flames die down.) Add the ginger and cinnamon, mix well, and cook 2 to 3 minutes longer. Let cool for about 5 minutes.

To serve: Run a knife around the sides of the ramekins, and turn each one over onto a plate to release the *panna cotta*. Top with about ¼ cup of the warm compote and a dollop of whipped cream. Garnish with a mint sprig.

CHERRY TART with STRAWBERRIES and DARK CHOCOLATE

SERVES 12

Choose medium-sized strawberries for the best presentation; large berries can make cutting the tart difficult. I sometimes melt a bit of white chocolate to drizzle over the top along with the dark chocolate, to make this an even showier dessert.

Crust

2 cups flour

$^1/_2$ cup confectioners' sugar

$^1/_2$ teaspoon pure vanilla extract

$^1/_2$ teaspoon salt

1 cup unsalted butter, cut into pieces

Cherry-Chocolate Filling

1 cup dry red wine

$^3/_4$ cup granulated sugar

1 cup dried cherries

1 cup mascarpone (page 190)

2 pints strawberries, rinsed and hulled

6 ounces bittersweet chocolate, chopped

1 tablespoon unsalted butter

1 cup heavy whipping cream, whipped, as an accompaniment

Mint sprigs, for garnish

To prepare the crust: Preheat the oven to 425°. Place the flour, sugar, vanilla, and salt in the bowl of a food processor. With the motor running, add the butter through the feed tube, a few pieces at a time, and process until a dough forms on top of the blades. Press the dough into a well-greased 10-inch tart or flan pan with a removable bottom. Bake until golden brown, about 15 minutes. Let cool completely.

To prepare the filling and assemble the tart: In a saucepan over high heat, combine the red wine, granulated sugar, and dried cherries, and cook until the cherries are tender and plump, 6 to 8 minutes. Let cool completely, then transfer to the bowl of a food processor and process until smooth. Add the mascarpone and process just until blended. Spread the filling over the prepared tart shell. Arrange the strawberries in concentric circles over the filling.

In the top of a double boiler, heat the chocolate and butter just until the chocolate has melted, and then stir to blend. Drizzle the chocolate over the strawberries. Refrigerate the tart for at least 2 hours, or up to 24 hours. Serve chilled, topped with whipped cream and garnished with mint sprigs.

CHOCOLATE VOLCANO BIRTHDAY CAKE

SERVES 12

I designed this cake with kids in mind. Its fun dome shape can be transformed into a flower, a ladybug, or a spider, and the filling is sweet and simple. If you prefer, bake it in standard cake pans instead of a bowl, and frost it with a traditional buttercream icing.

Chocolate Cake

1 cup unsalted butter, softened
1^1/$_2$ cups sugar
2 eggs
2 cups flour
^{3}/$_4$ cup cocoa powder, sifted
1 teaspoon baking soda
1 teaspoon baking powder
1^1/$_2$ cups sour cream

Cream Filling

1 cup heavy whipping cream
^{1}/$_4$ cup sugar
^{1}/$_2$ teaspoon pure vanilla extract

Chocolate Glaze

1 cup heavy whipping cream
12 ounces bittersweet chocolate, coarsely chopped

1 cup heavy whipping cream, whipped, as an
    accompaniment
Fresh edible flowers, such as pansies, lilacs, or
    nasturtiums, for garnish
Bittersweet chocolate shavings, for garnish

continued

To prepare the cake: Preheat the oven to 350°. In the bowl of a heavy-duty mixer, beat the butter and sugar until creamy and a pale yellow color. Beat in the eggs, one at a time, mixing well after each addition. Add 1 cup of the flour, the cocoa powder, baking soda, and baking powder, and beat well. Add the sour cream and beat well. Add the remaining flour and beat until smooth. Pour the batter into a well-greased 4-quart metal bowl and bake until a knife inserted in the cake comes out clean, 35 to 40 minutes. Let cool for 10 minutes, then flip the bowl over onto a rack to release the cake. Let cool completely.

To prepare the filling and fill the cake: Whip the cream, sugar, and vanilla until the cream holds soft peaks. Using a long, serrated knife, split the cake by cutting off a $^1/_2$-inch-thick slice from the cake's flat base. Turn the cake over so the flat side is facing up. Carefully scoop out the inside of the cake, setting aside 1 cup of cake crumbs, leaving a 1-inch-thick shell of cake all around. Gently fold the reserved cake crumbs into the whipped cream. Fill the hollowed-out cake with the whipped cream mixture, set the $^1/_2$-inch-thick base on top, and refrigerate for 1 hour.

To prepare the glaze: Heat the cream in a saucepan over high heat just until it comes to a boil. Meanwhile, place the chocolate in the bowl of a food processor and process until finely chopped. With the machine running, pour the hot cream through the feed tube and process until smooth. Transfer the glaze to a bowl and let cool for 10 minutes.

To glaze the cake: Place the cake, round side up, on a rack set in a baking sheet. Pour the glaze over the cake, letting it run down the sides to cover the cake completely. Refrigerate for at least 2 hours, or up to 24 hours.

To serve: Transfer the cake to a platter. Garnish with whipped cream, fresh flowers, and chocolate shavings.

SUMMER PUDDING

These puddings are perfect when entertaining in the heat of summer, since they require very little cooking. Although this dessert does not need a lot of preparation, it does require some advance planning, since the puddings must sit for at least 24 hours to soak up all the fruit juices.

3 cups raspberries, rinsed

1¹/₂ cups blackberries, rinsed

1 cup blueberries, rinsed

¹/₂ cup sugar

¹/₄ cup raspberry liqueur

¹/₂ teaspoon pure vanilla extract

1 teaspoon ground cinnamon

¹/₂ teaspoon ground ginger

¹/₂ teaspoon ground nutmeg

16 slices sweet egg bread, such as challah, or soft white bread

1 cup heavy whipping cream, whipped, as an accompaniment

In a large saucepan over high heat, combine the berries, sugar, liqueur, vanilla extract, cinnamon, ginger, and nutmeg. Bring to a boil and cook just until the sugar is dissolved, about 3 minutes. Let cool about 10 minutes.

Lightly grease eight 8-ounce ramekins. Using a ramekin as a guide, trim each slice of bread into a circle, discarding the crusts. Using a large slotted spoon, place a spoonful of the cooled berry mixture in each ramekin, then top with a circle of bread. Divide the remaining berry mixture among the ramekins. Top each with another circle of bread. Pour the remaining juice over each of the puddings to soak. Place the ramekins on a baking sheet, cover with plastic wrap, and top with a second baking sheet. Place 2 or 3 heavy cans on top to add weight. Refrigerate for 24 hours, or up to 2 days.

To serve, run a knife around the sides of the ramekins, and turn each one over onto a plate or pasta bowl to release the pudding. Top with a dollop of whipped cream.

CINNAMON POUND CAKE with MASCARPONE-COFFEE MERINGUE

The pound cake in this recipe can be made up to two days in advance. Let it cool completely, then wrap it tightly in plastic wrap and refrigerate for up to two days. The meringue is best served within two hours of being made. If you're not a fan of coffee, you can instead fold some diced poached pears into the meringue, or substitute almond or orange liqueur.

Cinnamon Pound Cake

1 cup unsalted butter, softened

2 cups granulated sugar

4 eggs

2 cups flour

1 teaspoon pure vanilla extract

1½ tablespoons ground cinnamon, toasted
    (page 186)

1 cup sour cream

Mascarpone-Coffee Meringue

1 cup mascarpone (page 190)

⅓ cup coffee liqueur

1 cup granulated sugar

1 tablespoon instant espresso powder or
    instant coffee

½ cup water

4 egg whites

½ cup cocoa powder, for dusting

½ cup confectioners' sugar, for dusting

Mint sprigs, for garnish

To prepare the pound cake: Preheat the oven to 350°. In the bowl of a heavy-duty mixer, beat the butter and granulated sugar at high speed until creamy and a pale lemon color, about 4 minutes. Add the eggs, one at a time, beating well after each one. Add half of the flour and beat well. Add the vanilla and cinnamon, and beat well. Add the sour cream and beat well. Add the remaining flour and beat well. Pour the batter into a well-greased 9-inch cake pan and bake until a knife inserted in the cake comes out clean, about 1 hour. Let cool for 10 minutes, then remove the cake from the pan. Set aside.

To prepare the coffee meringue: Combine the mascarpone and coffee liqueur in a bowl, and mix well. Set aside. In a small saucepan over high heat, combine the granulated sugar, espresso powder, and water. Bring the mixture to a boil and cook just until the mixture reaches the hard ball stage (about 250° on a candy thermometer). Let the syrup cool for about 5 minutes.

In the cleaned bowl of the mixer, whip the egg whites at high speed until they hold soft peaks. Slowly drizzle in the hot syrup, and continue whipping until the egg whites are very shiny and hold stiff peaks, about 5 minutes. Using broad strokes, gently fold the meringue into the mascarpone mixture.

To serve: Cut the cake into about 20 wedges. Place one wedge on each plate. Top with about 1/2 cup of the coffee meringue. Set another piece of cake on top of the meringue. Dust with cocoa powder and confectioners' sugar, and garnish with a mint sprig. Serve immediately.

PUMPKIN BREAD PUDDING with CANDIED PECAN TOPPING

For the holidays, try this bread pudding instead of traditional pumpkin pie. Its creamy custard and crispy spiced-nut topping will have even the most stuffed guests begging for more.

Candied Pecans
1 cup chopped pecans

$^1/_2$ cup brown sugar

2 tablespoons dark rum

1 tablespoon butter, melted

1 teaspoon ground cinnamon

1 teaspoon ground allspice

1 teaspoon ground ginger

Bread Pudding
5 cups diced French bread (about 1 loaf)

1 cup pumpkin purée

2 cups half-and-half

1 cup granulated sugar

5 eggs, lightly beaten

1 teaspoon pure vanilla extract

2 teaspoons ground cinnamon

1 teaspoon ground ginger

1 teaspoon ground allspice

1 teaspoon ground nutmeg

$^1/_2$ teaspoon ground cloves

Zest of 1 orange

1 cup heavy whipping cream, whipped, as an
   accompaniment

To prepare the candied pecans: Preheat the oven to 350°. Spread the pecans on a well-greased baking sheet and toast for 10 minutes. Meanwhile, in a bowl mix together the brown sugar, rum, butter, and spices. Add the pecans and toss well. Spread the mixture back on the baking sheet and bake 10 minutes longer, or until bubbly and caramelized. Let cool for 10 minutes, then remove them from the pan and let cool completely.

To prepare the bread pudding: Line a 10-inch springform pan with foil. Place the bread in the bottom of the pan. In a bowl, whisk together the pumpkin, half-and-half, and granulated sugar. Add the eggs, vanilla, spices, and orange zest, and whisk until smooth. Pour the pumpkin mixture over the bread and let stand 10 minutes. Spread the candied pecans over the top. Bake at 350° for about 45 minutes, or until a knife inserted in the bread pudding comes out clean. Let cool about 15 minutes.

To serve: Serve warm with whipped cream.

Other Things to Worry about Besides the Menu

Our customers come to the Bistro for the food and the wine, but all the other details—the staff and service, the lighting and furniture, the art and flowers—add up to their overall impression and enjoyment. It's no different when you want to make people comfortable in your home. When planning and preparing for guests, remember that sometimes subtle elements other than what you serve can have an impact on the success of your party. The following suggestions will help get you started.

- Decide on the type of party you want to have: formal, informal, indoor, outdoor, a special theme, and so on.

- Determine a budget for your party.

- Even if your party will be small, make sure you have enough plates, glasses, flatware, and other necessary equipment. If you're short on anything, make rental arrangements.

- If you're planning an outdoor party, consider seating and, if the party will be in the evening, the lighting.

- Have a backup plan for an outdoor party in case of bad weather.

- If you're hosting a sit-down dinner, set the table earlier in the day or even the night before.

- For a large or more elaborate party, make a to-do list to help you keep the details in focus.

- Make sure you have a designated place for coats and purses. (This may mean cleaning out a closet.)

- Prepare the guest bathroom.

- If you're having a large party, warn the neighbors.

MANGO TART with COCONUT-MACADAMIA CRUST

When John and I have friends over for dinner, the meal often has an Asian touch. To finish the evening, I like to serve this tart—it's not only exotic, but it also provides a cooling effect that is welcome after the chiles and ginger.

Coconut-Macadamia Crust

1¹/₂ cups ground toasted macadamia nuts (page 186)

¹/₂ cup grated fresh coconut

¹/₂ teaspoon ground ginger

¹/₄ cup sugar

6 tablespoons unsalted butter, melted

Mango Filling

6 mangoes, peeled and diced

1 cup sugar

1 teaspoon pure vanilla extract

1 teaspoon cornstarch

Pinch five-spice powder

1 teaspoon ground cinnamon

¹/₂ teaspoon ground ginger

Zest of 1 lime

2 tablespoons dark rum

1 cup heavy whipping cream, whipped, as an accompaniment

To prepare the crust: In a large bowl, combine the macadamia nuts, coconut, ginger, and sugar, and mix well. Add the melted butter, and mix well. Press the mixture into a well-greased 10-inch tart or flan pan with a removable bottom. Refrigerate.

To prepare the filling and bake the tart: Preheat the oven to 375°. Place the mangoes in a bowl. Add the sugar, vanilla, cornstarch, five-spice powder, cinnamon, ginger, lime zest, and dark rum, and mix well. Pour the filling into the crust. Bake until the filling bubbles and the sugar is dissolved, about 40 minutes. Let cool for about 20 minutes.

To serve: Serve warm with whipped cream.

CHOCOLATE MOUSSE with SPICE-POACHED PEARS

Both the mousse and the pears for this great fall dessert can be prepared up to two days in advance. Store the pears in their poaching liquid, and be sure to place them on top of the mousse no more than four hours before serving. A quick caramelization is all they'll need at the last minute. Although a propane torch is a tool more often found in the garage than the kitchen, I prefer to use it because it gives me much more control than the broiler.

Chocolate Mousse

12 ounces bittersweet chocolate, chopped

2 tablespoons unsalted butter

$1/4$ cup pear brandy

4 eggs, separated

1 cup heavy whipping cream

Poached Pears

1 cup dry white wine

$1/2$ cup sugar

1 cinnamon stick

2 whole cloves

4 pears, peeled, cored, and halved

1 cup sugar, for the tops

1 cup heavy whipping cream, whipped, as an accompaniment

To prepare the mousse: Place the chocolate, butter, and brandy in the top of a double boiler, and heat until the chocolate has melted about halfway. Remove from the heat and let the chocolate finish melting. Stir and let cool 5 minutes. Whisk in the egg yolks. Whip the cream to soft peaks, and gently fold it into the chocolate mixture. In the bowl of a heavy-duty mixer, whip the egg whites at high speed until they hold soft peaks. Gently fold the egg whites into the chocolate mixture. Divide the mousse among eight 8-ounce ramekins. Refrigerate.

To prepare the pears: Combine the wine, sugar, cinnamon, and cloves in a saucepan over high heat, and bring to a boil. Place the pears in the poaching liquid and poach until tender, 5 to 7 minutes. Drain the pears well and slice.

To serve: Top each ramekin of mousse with one-half of a sliced pear and sprinkle with 2 tablespoons sugar. Place the ramekins under a very hot broiler and broil until the sugar is caramelized, about 1 minute. Alternatively, use a propane torch to caramelize the sugar. Top with whipped cream and serve immediately.

NOTE: Children and individuals who are immunosuppressed should not eat uncooked eggs that have not been pasteurized.

LEMON PANCAKES with RASPBERRY COMPOTE

SERVES 8

These were a big hit with our students during our summer cooking class series, although at first many thought the idea of using pancakes as a dessert sounded a bit odd. But when I used the pancakes to line dessert bowls and filled them with the warm compote and ice cream, all we heard—besides spoons scraping the bottoms of bowls—was "Mmm!" You'll receive the same compliment from your guests. You can modify the presentation and dress the dish up or down to suit any occasion; I've used everything from simple coffee cups to cut crystal bowls as serving dishes.

Raspberry Compote

2 tablespoons unsalted butter
3 pints raspberries, rinsed
¹/₂ cup sugar
Juice of ¹/₂ lemon
¹/₃ cup raspberry liqueur

Lemon Pancakes

1 cup flour
1 cup milk
2 eggs
2 tablespoons sugar
Grated zest of 1 lemon
Juice of ¹/₂ lemon
1 teaspoon ground ginger
2 tablespoons butter, melted

1 pint high-quality vanilla ice cream, as an accompaniment
1 cup heavy whipping cream, whipped, as an accompaniment
Mint sprigs, for garnish

To prepare the compote: Heat the butter in a saucepan over high heat until melted and bubbly. Add the raspberries and stir. Add the sugar and lemon juice and cook, stirring occasionally, until the sugar dissolves, 3 to 4 minutes. Add the liqueur and cook just until the compote comes to a boil. Keep warm over low heat, or refrigerate and reheat before serving. (The compote can be prepared in advance and kept refrigerated for up to 1 day.)

To prepare the pancakes: Place the flour in a bowl and slowly whisk in the milk. Add the eggs and whisk well. Add the sugar, lemon zest and juice, ginger, and butter, and whisk until smooth (thin with additional milk if needed). Brush an 8-inch nonstick sauté pan over high heat with about $1/2$ teaspoon of vegetable oil, and heat until very hot. Pour in $1/4$ cup of the batter, swirling the pan to create a thin, even pancake. Cook until the batter bubbles, about 2 minutes, and then flip the pancake and cook about 1 minute longer. Remove the pancake from the pan, and set aside. Repeat with the remaining batter.

To serve: Set each pancake inside a dessert dish or small bowl (to line the dish). Add about $1/2$ cup of the warm compote. Top with a scoop of vanilla ice cream and a dollop of whipped cream. Garnish with a sprig of mint. Serve warm.

BOURBON-SOAKED BABAS with MARINATED FRUIT

Babas are made from a yeasted dough that lies somewhere between cake and bread. Once soaked with syrup, pillowy soft babas literally melt in your mouth, creating a memorable finish to an evening. Although the babas need to be baked and soaked just before serving, both the marinated fruit and the syrup can be made up to 24 hours in advance. Don't limit the syrup to just bourbon—any of your favorite liquors will work.

Marinated Fruit

2 cups seasonal fruit, diced if necessary

2 tablespoons sugar, or more to taste

Dash pure vanilla extract

1 teaspoon chopped fresh mint

$^{1}/_{2}$ teaspoon ground cinnamon

Bourbon Syrup

1 cup sugar

2 cups water

$^{1}/_{4}$ cup bourbon

Babas

6 tablespoons warm water

$1^{1}/_{2}$ teaspoons yeast

1 teaspoon sugar

1 egg

$^{3}/_{4}$ cup flour

Grated zest of 1 orange

2 tablespoons unsalted butter, softened

$^{1}/_{2}$ cup heavy whipping cream, whipped, as an accompaniment

To marinate the fruit: Combine the fruit, sugar, vanilla, mint, and cinnamon in a bowl and mix well. Let the fruit marinate for at least 30 minutes, or up to 24 hours.

To prepare the syrup: In a saucepan over high heat, combine the sugar, water, and bourbon, and bring to a boil. Boil for 2 to 3 minutes, remove the pan from the heat, and set aside, or refrigerate for up to 1 week.

To prepare the babas: In the bowl of a heavy-duty mixer, combine the water, yeast, and sugar and mix just to combine. Let it sit until foamy, about 5 minutes. Add the egg, flour, orange zest, and butter and mix until elastic but very soft. Let the dough rise in a warm place until it doubles in volume, 15 to 20 minutes. Punch the dough down. Spoon the dough into greased muffin tins, filling them one-third to one-half full. Let the dough rise again until doubled in volume, 20 to 30 minutes.

While the babas are rising, preheat the oven to 350°. Bake the babas until golden brown, about 15 minutes. Remove from the tins and place on a cooling rack set over a baking sheet. Prick the tops of the babas with a skewer or fork. Warm the syrup over medium heat. Ladle all of the warm syrup over the babas, letting it soak in.

To serve: Place the babas on individual plates. Distribute the fruit among the babas, and top with whipped cream. Serve warm.

DEEP-FRIED COCONUT PÂTE À CHOUX

SERVES 6

This impressive dessert is simple to prepare, especially if you do some of the steps ahead of time. The dough can be made up to two days in advance and then piped out when ready to use. You can deep-fry the pâte à choux *two hours before serving, then warm for about five minutes in a 350° oven. The chocolate sauce can also be made up to a week in advance.*

Coconut Pâte à Choux

1 cup coconut milk

¹/₂ cup unsalted butter, diced

¹/₂ teaspoon pure vanilla extract

1 cup flour

6 eggs

¹/₂ cup finely chopped fresh coconut

Chocolate Sauce

1¹/₄ cups heavy whipping cream

10 ounces bittersweet chocolate, chopped

¹/₄ cup coffee liqueur

2 tablespoons unsalted butter

Vegetable oil, for deep-frying

1 pint high-quality vanilla ice cream, as an accompaniment

¹/₄ cup toasted fresh coconut, for garnish

Mint sprigs, for garnish

To prepare the *pâte à choux:* In a saucepan over high heat, combine the coconut milk, butter, and vanilla. Bring the mixture to a boil. Whisk in the flour, decrease the heat to low, and cook, stirring often, for 5 minutes to dry the dough. Transfer the mixture to the bowl of a heavy-duty mixer. With the mixer on high speed, add the eggs, one at a time, and beat until smooth. Add the coconut, and mix well.

Transfer the dough to a large pastry bag fitted with a medium star tip. Pipe the dough into six 4-inch circles on a greased baking sheet. Refrigerate for 30 minutes to chill.

To prepare the chocolate sauce: Heat the cream, chocolate, and liqueur in a heavy saucepan over medium heat until the chocolate is melted. Remove from the heat, add the butter, and whisk until smooth. Set aside for up to 1 hour, or refrigerate.

To deep-fry the *pâte à choux:* Heat 6 inches of vegetable oil in a large saucepan over high heat until it reaches 350°. Add 2 or 3 of the chilled *pâte à choux* circles and cook until golden brown, 6 to 8 minutes. Transfer to paper towels to drain. Repeat with the remaining *pâte à choux.*

To serve: Warm the chocolate sauce over low heat. Place each cooked pastry on a plate, fill with a scoop of vanilla ice cream, top with warm chocolate sauce, sprinkle with toasted coconut, and garnish with a mint sprig.

CARAMELIZED STRAWBERRIES with BAKED MERINGUE

SERVES 6

Small, sweet ruby-red Oregon strawberries are my favorites, and this recipe really shows them off. Floating in a rich syrup, they make a wonderful contrast to the light, fluffy meringue on top. Although this dessert requires last-minute finishing, you can prepare the strawberries up to two hours in advance, and then cover them and leave them at room temperature. To serve, make the meringue, top the berries, and bake.

1 cup granulated sugar
$1/4$ cup water
3 pints strawberries, rinsed, hulled, and halved
2 tablespoons Grand Marnier
2 tablespoons unsalted butter
4 egg whites
1 cup brown sugar

To prepare the strawberries: Combine the granulated sugar and water in a 4-quart Dutch oven or large ovenproof sauté pan over high heat and cook, without stirring, until the sugar starts to brown, about 10 minutes. Swirl the pan to even the brown color. Add the strawberries and Grand Marnier and cook just until the strawberries are tender and the sugar has completely melted, about 5 minutes. Add the butter and stir until melted. Let cool.

To prepare the meringue: Preheat the oven to 425°. In the bowl of a heavy-duty mixer, whip the egg whites at high speed until very foamy. Slowly add the brown sugar, about 1 tablespoon at a time, and continue whipping until the egg whites are very shiny and hold a stiff peak, about 5 minutes. Spread the meringue over the cooked strawberries. Bake until golden brown, 10 to 12 minutes.

To serve: Scoop the berries into bowls. Serve warm.

LIME-COCONUT CHESS PIE

I often like to finish my parties on a simple, satisfying note, rather than trying to chase the hottest dessert trend. Chess pie, for example, is a simple, old-fashioned Southern dessert. The basic pie has led to many variations, such as this one with lime and coconut.

Crust

1¹/₃ cups flour
¹/₄ cup shortening
¹/₄ unsalted butter, diced
1 teaspoon salt
6 tablespoons cold water

Lime-Coconut Filling

1¹/₃ cups sugar
¹/₂ cup unsalted butter, melted
4 eggs
¹/₂ teaspoon pure vanilla extract
Grated zest and juice of 1 lime
1 cup sweetened flaked coconut

1 cup heavy whipping cream, whipped, as an accompaniment
¹/₂ cup toasted fresh coconut, for garnish

To prepare the crust: Preheat the oven to 350°. Place the flour, shortening, butter, and salt in a bowl. Using your fingertips, mix until the dough resembles a coarse meal. Add the water and mix with a fork just until the dough comes together. Roll the dough into a ball and wrap tightly with plastic wrap. Let rest 15 minutes. (The dough can be prepared in advance and kept refrigerated for up to 4 days, or frozen for up to 6 months.) On a well-floured board, roll the dough out into a 10-inch circle. Place the dough in a 9-inch pie plate and flute the edges. Set aside.

To prepare the filling and bake the pie: Combine the sugar and butter in the bowl of a food processor, and process until thick and creamy. With the machine running, add the eggs, one at a time, through the feed tube and process until smooth. Add the vanilla and the lime zest and juice, and process until the batter is well blended. Sprinkle the coconut over the bottom of the crust. Pour the batter over the coconut. Bake until just set and a knife inserted in the pie comes out clean, 25 to 30 minutes. Let cool for about 10 minutes before serving, or refrigerate for up to 24 hours.

To serve: Serve warm or chilled, topped with whipped cream and toasted coconut.

RHUBARB CRÈME BRÛLÉE

SERVES 8

Rhubarb is the much-anticipated first fresh, local "fruit" we get at the restaurant in the spring. It always makes its way into crème brûlée, a staple of the Bistro's dessert menu. I really like to serve brûlées for dinner parties, because I can make the custards up to a week in advance and simply caramelize them before serving. My guests are always impressed!

2 tablespoons unsalted butter

3 cups diced rhubarb

2¹/₂ cups sugar

¹/₂ teaspoon ground cinnamon

4 cups half-and-half

1 vanilla bean, split in half lengthwise

1 tablespoon diced candied ginger

8 egg yolks

To prepare the rhubarb: Heat the butter in a large sauté pan over high heat until very hot. Add the rhubarb, 1 cup of the sugar, and the cinnamon, and sauté until very tender, about 5 minutes. Divide the rhubarb among eight 8-ounce ramekins. Set aside.

To prepare the custard: Preheat the oven to 325°. In a saucepan over medium heat, combine the half-and-half, vanilla bean, and candied ginger, and bring just to a boil. Remove the pan from heat; scrape seeds from the center of the vanilla bean into the custard, and then discard the bean. Meanwhile, in a large bowl, whisk together ¹/₂ cup of the sugar and the egg yolks. When the half-and-half is hot, whisk 1 cup of it into the egg mixture. Pour the egg mixture into the remaining half-and-half, and whisk until smooth. Using a large spoon, skim the foam from the surface of the custard. Divide the custard among the ramekins.

To bake the custard: Place the ramekins in a roasting pan, and fill the pan with enough hot water to reach about halfway up the sides of the ramekins. Carefully set the pan in the oven and bake until the custard is set, about 50 minutes. Remove the ramekins from the roasting pan. Let the custards cool for at least 2 hours.

To serve: Sprinkle each custard with 2 tablespoons of the remaining sugar. Place the ramekins under a very hot broiler and broil until the sugar is caramelized, about 1 minute. Or use a propane torch to caramelize the sugar. Serve immediately.

Roasted Shallot Shmear / 185

Roasted Shallots / 185

Fried Shallots / 185

Roasted Garlic / 185

Smoked Onions / 185

Toasted Bread Crumbs / 185

Toasted Spices and Sesame Seeds / 186

Toasted Nuts and Seeds / 186

Skinned Hazelnuts / 186

Roasted and Pulverized Dried Chiles / 186

Roasted Bell Peppers and Chiles / 186

Cooked Lobster / 186

Fish Stock / 186

Chicken Stock / 187

Veal Stock / 187

Shrimp Stock / 187

Vegetable Stock / 188

Blanched and Shocked Vegetables / 188

Simple Tomato Sauce / 188

Seeded Tomatoes / 188

Peeled Tomatoes and Peaches / 189

Cooked Basmati Rice / 189

Béchamel Sauce / 189

Balsamic Syrup / 189

Mascarpone / 190

Crème Fraîche / 190

Puff Pastry / 190

basics

ROASTED SHALLOT SHMEAR

MAKES 1¹/₂ CUPS

10 whole shallots, peeled and halved

10 cloves garlic

¹/₄ cup extra virgin olive oil

¹/₄ cup balsamic vinegar

2 anchovies ~ NOT USED

2 tablespoons chopped fresh rosemary

Salt

Freshly ground black pepper

Preheat the oven to 300°. Place the shallots and garlic in an ovenproof pan, drizzle with the olive oil, and roast until the shallots are soft to the touch, 50 minutes to 1 hour. Transfer the mixture to the bowl of a food processor, add the vinegar, anchovies, and rosemary and purée until smooth. Season to taste with salt and pepper, and process briefly to mix. The shmear will keep refrigerated for up to 1 week. Refrigerate until ready to use.

ROASTED SHALLOTS

Roasted shallots will keep in the refrigerator for up to two weeks.

6 shallots, peeled

¹/₄ cup extra virgin olive oil

Preheat the oven to 250°. Place the shallots in a small baking dish, drizzle with the olive oil, and roast until soft, 40 to 50 minutes.

FRIED SHALLOTS

MAKES ABOUT ¹/₂ CUP

¹/₄ cup extra virgin olive oil

6 shallots, julienned

Heat the olive oil in a large sauté pan over high heat until very hot. Add the shallots and cook until crisp and golden brown, 4 to 5 minutes. Transfer to a paper towel to drain.

ROASTED GARLIC

1 head garlic

2 tablespoons extra virgin olive oil

Preheat the oven to 250°. Slice about ¹/₄ inch off the top of the garlic head and discard. Drizzle the garlic with the olive oil and wrap tightly in foil. Roast until soft, 40 to 50 minutes. Squeeze each clove to remove the roasted garlic from the papery outer layer. Roasted garlic will keep in the refrigerator for 2 to 3 weeks.

SMOKED ONIONS

Smoking is an easy process that can be done up to five days before you want to use the onions. Use large yellow onions.

Prepare coals by piling briquettes on one side of the barbecue and lighting them. Let them burn until they are gray in color. Meanwhile, peel the onions and cut them in half. Remove the grill from the barbecue and oil it well. Place smoking chips (alder, apple, grapevines, tea, or any type of hardwood) on the coals, and set the grill back on the barbecue. Place the onions cut side down on the opposite side of the grill from the coals. Cover the barbecue and let the onions smoke for 1 to 2 hours, adding more chips if the smoke dies down. The onions should be nicely browned and have a lightly smoked aroma.

TOASTED BREAD CRUMBS

MAKES ABOUT 2 CUPS

5 slices white bread

Preheat the oven to 350°. Remove the crusts from the bread and discard. Tear the bread into pieces, place them in a food processor and process to fine crumbs. Place the crumbs on a baking sheet and toast until golden brown, about 10 minutes.

TOASTED SPICES and SESAME SEEDS

Heat a dry skillet over medium-high heat until hot. Add the whole or ground spices or sesame seeds and toast while stirring continuously. Toast whole spices for about 2 minutes, ground spices for 3 to 5 minutes, or until lightly browned and aromatic. Remove from the heat and set aside to cool.

TOASTED NUTS and SEEDS

Preheat oven to 350°. Place the nuts or seeds on a baking sheet and toast for about 10 minutes, or until golden brown and aromatic. Let cool completely, and then use as directed.

SKINNED HAZELNUTS

Toast the hazelnuts as directed above, then wrap in a kitchen towel and set aside to cool. When completedly cool, leave the nuts wrapped in the towel and vigorously roll them between your palms until most of the skins have been removed. (It is not necessary to remove all the skins.) Use as directed.

ROASTED and PULVERIZED DRIED CHILES

Preheat oven to 350°. Place the dried chiles on a baking sheet and bake until puffy and dark brown, about 12 minutes. Let cool. Remove and discard the stems and seeds. Using a coffee or spice grinder, grind the chiles to a fine powder.

ROASTED BELL PEPPERS and CHILES

Preheat the broiler. Place the peppers or chiles on a baking sheet and broil, turning until the skins are evenly blistered and charred, for about 15 minutes. Transfer to a bowl, cover with plastic wrap, and set aside to cool. When the peppers are cool enough to handle, peel off the skins, remove the stems, and wipe the seeds away. Do not rinse the peppers or chiles under running water because this washes away much of the roasted flavor. Use as directed, or drizzle with olive oil and store in an airtight container in the refrigerator for up to 2 months.

COOKED LOBSTER

6 cups water

1 lemon, halved

1 bay leaf

5 sprigs thyme

3 cloves garlic, peeled

1 live lobster

In a large stockpot over high heat, combine the water, lemon, bay leaf, thyme, and garlic. Bring the water to a rolling boil. Plunge the lobster into the water and boil until just cooked through and pink, about 10 minutes. Immediately transfer the lobster to an ice water bath to stop the cooking process. Remove the lobster meat from the shell.

FISH STOCK

MAKES ABOUT 4 CUPS

1 pound fish bones (use bones from whitefish only)

1 tablespoon unsalted butter

2 leeks, white part only, rinsed well and coarsely chopped

2 large onions, coarsely chopped

2 stalks celery, coarsely chopped

2 cloves garlic, chopped

$1/4$ cup mushroom stems

1 cup dry white wine

4 sprigs thyme

8 cups cold water

Coarsely chop the fish bones and place them in a large bowl or stockpot. Cover with cold water and soak for 1 or 2 hours to remove any remaining traces of blood. Drain.

Heat the butter in a large stockpot over high heat until melted. Add the leeks, onions, celery, garlic, and mushroom stems, and sauté for 3 to 4 minutes. Add the wine and bones, lower heat to medium-low, cover the pot, and sweat the mixture for 8 minutes. Add the thyme and water and simmer, uncovered, for 25 minutes. Strain through a fine sieve into a bowl and use immediately, or let cool to room temperature before refrigerating. Keep refrigerated for up to 1 week, or frozen for up to 6 months.

CHICKEN STOCK

MAKES ABOUT 4 CUPS

 2 pounds chicken bones, rinsed
 2 onions, coarsely chopped
 2 carrots, coarsely chopped
 2 stalks celery, coarsely chopped
 3 cloves garlic, chopped
 4 sprigs thyme
 8 cups water
 1 bay leaf

In a large stockpot over high heat, combine the bones, onions, carrots, celery, garlic, thyme, and water, and bring just to a boil. Add the bay leaf, reduce heat to low, and simmer for 4 to 6 hours, or until the stock is richly flavored. Strain through a fine sieve and use immediately, or let cool to room temperature before refrigerating. Keep refrigerated for up to 1 week, or frozen for up to 6 months.

VEAL STOCK

MAKES ABOUT 4 CUPS

 5 pounds veal bones
 2 onions, coarsely chopped

 1 carrot, coarsely chopped
 3 stalks celery, coarsely chopped
 3 cloves garlic, chopped
 2 tablespoons tomato paste
 1 cup dry red wine
 8 cups water
 1 bay leaf

Preheat the oven to 450°. Place the bones, onions, carrot, celery, and garlic in a roasting pan, and roast for 1 hour, or until the bones are browned. Spread the tomato paste over the mixture and roast for 10 minutes longer. Transfer mixture to a large stockpot. Add the wine to the roasting pan and scrape the bottom of the pan to deglaze. Pour the wine mixture into the stockpot. Add the water and bay leaf, and bring to a boil. Decrease the heat to low and simmer for 6 to 8 hours, or until the stock is richly flavored. Strain through a fine sieve and use immediately, or let cool to room temperature before refrigerating. Keep refrigerated for up to 1 week, or frozen for up to 6 months.

SHRIMP STOCK

MAKES ABOUT 4 CUPS

 1 tablespoon unsalted butter
 2 leeks, white parts only, rinsed well and coarsely chopped
 2 large onions, coarsely chopped
 2 stalks celery, coarsely chopped
 2 cloves garlic, chopped
 $1/4$ cup mushroom stems
 1 cup dry white wine
 6 cups shrimp shells
 4 sprigs thyme
 8 cups water

Heat the butter in a large stockpot over high heat until melted. Add the leeks, onions, celery, garlic, and mushroom stems, and sauté for 3 to

4 minutes. Add the wine and shells, decrease the heat to medium-low, cover the pot, and sweat the mixture for about 8 minutes. Add the thyme and water and simmer, uncovered, for 25 minutes. Strain through a fine sieve and use immediately, or let cool to room temperature before refrigerating. Keep refrigerated for up to 1 week, or frozen for up to 6 months.

VEGETABLE STOCK

MAKES ABOUT 4 CUPS

  3 onions, coarsely chopped
  4 carrots, coarsely chopped
  5 stalks celery, coarsely chopped
  4 ounces mushrooms, coarsely chopped
  4 cloves garlic, chopped
  3 shallots, chopped
  6 sprigs thyme
  8 cups water

Combine all the ingredients in a large stockpot over high heat and bring just to a boil. Decrease the heat to low and simmer for about 1 hour, or until the stock is richly flavored. Strain through a fine sieve into a bowl and use immediately, or let cool to room temperature before refrigerating. Keep refrigerated for up to 1 week, or frozen for up to 6 months.

NOTE: To make **roasted vegetable stock**, place all the vegetables in a large baking dish and roast in a 425° oven for 20 minutes. Add the roasted vegetables to the stockpot of boiling water and proceed as directed above.

BLANCHED and SHOCKED VEGETABLES

Bring a pot of water to a boil over high heat. Add the vegetables and cook until crisp-tender. Drain immediately and transfer to a large bowl of ice water to stop the cooking process. Use as directed.

SIMPLE TOMATO SAUCE

MAKES ABOUT 3 CUPS

The sauce will keep refrigerated for up to one week.

  1 tablespoon extra virgin olive oil
  3 cloves garlic, chopped
  2 shallots, chopped
  4 cups peeled, seeded, and diced tomatoes
    (pages 188 and 189)
  1 cup red wine
  1 cup vegetable stock (this page) or chicken stock
    (page 187)
  Salt
  Freshly ground black pepper

Heat the olive oil in a large saucepan over high heat until very hot. Add the garlic and shallots and sauté for 2 minutes. Add the tomatoes and wine, and reduce until the mixture is almost dry, about 5 minutes. Add the stock and reduce until about $1/4$ cup of stock remains, about 8 minutes. Using a blender or hand-held blender, purée the sauce until smooth. Pour the sauce back into the pan and simmer over medium-low heat for about 5 minutes. Season to taste with salt and pepper.

SEEDED TOMATOES

Cut the tomatoes in half crosswise. Cup one tomato half in the palm of your hand and squeeze gently until the seeds spill out.

PEELED TOMATOES and PEACHES

Bring a stockpot of water to a boil. Cut an X in the bottom of each tomato or peach. Add the whole tomatoes or peaches to the stockpot and blanch briefly, about 1 minute. Using a slotted spoon, immediately transfer the tomatoes or peaches to a large bowl of ice water. When the tomatoes or peaches are cool, peel them. The skins should slip off easily.

COOKED BASMATI RICE

MAKES ABOUT 2 CUPS

2 teaspoons vegetable oil

2 cloves garlic, chopped

2 teaspoons peeled, chopped fresh ginger

1 cup basmati rice, rinsed until the water runs clear

2 cups chicken stock (page 187) or vegetable stock (page 188)

Salt

Freshly ground black pepper

Preheat the oven to 350°. Heat the oil in an ovenproof saucepan over high heat until very hot. Add the garlic and ginger, and sauté for 2 minutes. Add the rice, stir to coat it well with the oil, and sauté for about 2 minutes. Add the stock and season well with salt and pepper. Bring the mixture to a boil, cover the pan with a lid, and place it in the oven. Bake for 15 minutes. Stir well, cover, and bake 15 minutes longer, or until the rice is tender. Serve warm.

BÉCHAMEL SAUCE

MAKES ABOUT 2 CUPS

The sauce will keep refrigerated for up to one week.

1 whole clove

One-fourth of a yellow onion

2 cups milk

1 clove garlic, chopped

Pinch nutmeg

2 tablespoons unsalted butter, softened

3 tablespoons flour

Salt

Freshly ground black pepper

Press the clove into the onion quarter. In a saucepan over medium heat, combine the milk, garlic, nutmeg, and onion, and heat the mixture until just under a boil. Meanwhile, in a small bowl, mix together the butter and flour until a soft dough forms. Quickly whisk the butter mixture into the milk and cook, whisking often, until the sauce thickens, about 3 minutes. Season to taste with salt and pepper. Strain the sauce through a fine sieve and keep warm.

BALSAMIC SYRUP

MAKES ABOUT 2 TABLESPOONS

Balsamic syrup will keep refrigerated for up to two weeks.

1 17-ounce bottle balsamic vinegar (aged for at least 5 years)

In a heavy-duty saucepan over medium-low heat, reduce the balsamic vinegar until 2 tablespoons of liquid remain, about 20 minutes.

MASCARPONE

MAKES 1 CUP

2 cups heavy whipping cream

1 teaspoon tartaric acid (available at home wine-
making supply shops)

In a saucepan over high heat, whisk together the cream and tartaric acid, and bring just to a boil. Remove from the heat and let cool for about 10 minutes. Transfer the mixture to a strainer lined with several layers of cheesecloth, set the strainer over a bowl, and let it sit in the refrigerator overnight. Remove the chilled mascarpone from the cheesecloth until ready to use (discard the liquid in the bowl). The mascarpone will keep refrigerated for up to 1 week.

CRÈME FRAÎCHE

2 cups heavy whipping cream

2 tablespoons sour cream

In a small bowl, whisk together the whipping cream and sour cream. Cover and let sit at room temperature for 8 hours or overnight, then refrigerate until thickened. The crème fraîche will keep, refrigerated, for up to 1 week.

PUFF PASTRY

4$^1/_2$ cups flour

2 cups unsalted butter, diced

1 teaspoon salt

1 cup plus 2 tablespoons cold water

Place the flour, butter, and salt in a large bowl. Using your fingertips, mix the butter with the flour until it resembles a coarse meal. (It's all right if there are some large pieces of butter.) Add about 1 cup of the water and mix with a fork just until it comes together.

Transfer the dough to a well-floured board and form it into a rough rectangle. Fold one-third of the dough toward the center. Fold the other third over toward the center. Turn the dough 90 degrees. Sprinkle the dough with flour and roll it out into a 20 by 6-inch rectangle. Fold the dough in thirds again. Turn it 90 degrees, sprinkle with flour, and roll it out again. Repeat the process two more times.

Cover the dough with plastic wrap and refrigerate for at least 1 hour. Use as directed. (The dough can be cut into smaller pieces, wrapped, and kept frozen for up to 6 months.)

Glossary

Arugula: Also called rocket, arugula is a tender green with a nutty, spicy flavor. I like to add it to salads, sandwiches, and pastas.

Blanch: To partially cook briefly in boiling water or hot oil.

Bok choy (and baby bok choy): Also called Chinese white cabbage, bok choy is a dark green cabbage that somewhat resembles Swiss chard; baby bok choy is a smaller, more tender variety.

Butterfly: To cut a piece of meat nearly all the way through and open it out to make it twice as long but half as thick as it originally was. The meat should then be pounded flat with a meat mallet.

Caramelize: To cook sugar or an ingredient with a naturally high sugar content (such as some vegetables, fruits, and meats) over high heat to brown the natural sugars and develop a deeper flavor.

Cayenne sauce: A vinegar-based, tangy, spicy sauce. I like to add it to soups, sauces, marinades, and salsas.

Chile paste: A Chinese condiment made from fermented fava beans, red chiles, and, sometimes, garlic.

Crème fraîche: Cream combined with sour cream (or buttermilk) that is left out at room temperature for 8 to 24 hours, then refrigerated until thickened.

Crystallized ginger: Also known as candied ginger. Available in most grocery stores and Asian markets.

Curry paste: A mixture of ghee (clarified butter), vinegar, and curry powder used to flavor Indian and Asian dishes. Sold in gourmet and specialty shops.

Emulsify: To completely blend together an oil or fat with an acid such as vinegar or lemon juice.

Fermented black beans: Small black soybeans preserved with salt that are widely used in Chinese cooking. They have a distinct pungency and strong salty taste. I rinse them before using.

Fish sauce: A thin sauce made from fermented salted sardines or other fish.

Hoisin: A Chinese sauce made with sugar, vinegar, soybeans, and spices.

Julienne: To cut into matchsticks about $1/8$ inch across by 2 inches long.

Kalamata olives: Smooth-skinned, dark purple, brine-cured Greek olives with an intense taste.

Kosher salt: Pure salt with an even, coarse texture; more soluble than table salt. Available in specialty markets and most grocery stores.

Lemongrass: A standard herb in Vietnamese and Thai cooking. Use fresh lemongrass for cooking; dried lemongrass is mainly used for tea. Available in Asian markets and some grocery stores.

Mesclun: Mixed wild salad greens.

Nonreactive bowl/pan/container: Made of glass, ceramic, or stainless steel. Metal components in aluminum and cast iron can react with the acids in ingredients, resulting in an off flavor.

Pancetta: Unsmoked Italian bacon. Available in gourmet markets.

Parchment paper: Oil- and moisture-resistant paper used to line baking sheets and pans to prevent baked items from sticking.

Pickled ginger: A common Japanese condiment, it consists of very thinly sliced ginger pickled in rice vinegar, salt, and spices. Commercial varieties are artificially colored.

Prosciutto: Dry-cured, spiced Italian ham available in gourmet markets.

Reduce: To thicken and intensify the flavor of liquid by boiling it down.

Shock: To submerge briefly in ice-cold water to stop the cooking process.

Soba noodles: Japanese buckwheat noodles.

Sweet soy sauce: A sweet, syrup-like Indonesian soy sauce; also called *kecap manis.*

Tahini: A paste made from toasted sesame seeds that is used in Middle Eastern cooking.

Tamarind pulp: Sweet-sour paste made from the fruit of the pods of the tamarind tree.

Tapenade: A thick paste made from capers, anchovies, black olives, olive oil, and lemon juice.

Thai basil: A basil variety with green and maroon leaves that has a slightly spicy flavor.

Wasabi: Japanese green mustard, with similar flavor and usages as horseradish. Wasabi is very hot and pungent, and should be used sparingly. Available in powder and paste form in Asian markets and some grocery stores.

Wild mushrooms: All edible, nonpoisonous mushrooms that are indigenous throughout the Pacific Northwest, among other regions. Some of the most common are chanterelles, enoki, morels, and shiitakes, which are all known for their particularly earthy qualities.

A CHILD'S BIRTHDAY PARTY

Mini Pizza Turnovers

Corn Dogs

Chocolate Volcano Birthday Cake

CHRISTMAS BREAKFAST

Dried Cherry Coffee Cake

Crab Frittata

Marinated Melon Wedges

Oven Home Fries

A NEW YEAR'S EVE PARTY

Wild Mushroom Tarte Tatin

Chilled Five-Spice Prawns with Caper Aioli

Oyster Stew

Oven-Roasted Goat Cheese Salad with Arugula

Chocolate Mousse with Spice-Poached Pears

TUSCAN-INSPIRED DINNER

Marinated Sweet Peppers

Tuscan-Style Roasted Game Hens

Panna Cotta with Blackberry Compote

A COCKTAIL OR WINE-TASTING PARTY

Sesame-Cheddar Crackers

Roasted Baby New Potatoes with Olive Tapenade

Smoked Salmon Pizza

Marinated Olives

Fava Bean Bruschetta

Marinated Sweet Peppers

Tomato-Basil Tart

menus

A COZY SUNDAY DINNER

Green Onion–Buttermilk Biscuits

Roasted Pork Loin with Rosemary-Balsamic Glaze

The Best Mashed Potatoes

Creamy Garlic Spinach

Lime-Coconut Chess Pie

A VEGETARIAN DINNER

Eggplant and Blue Cheese Spread with toasted baguette slices

Sweet Potato and Mushroom Soufflés

Spinach Salad with Pear-Thyme Vinaigrette

Seared Apples with Brandy-Vanilla Syrup

A ROMANTIC DINNER

One-Minute Salmon with Lemongrass-Soy Aioli

Poached Seabass with Roasted Yellow Pepper–Yogurt Sauce

Mark's Jungle Rice

Sautéed Baby Bok Choy with Toasted Sesame Sauce

Silky Chocolate-Raspberry Tart

A SUMMER BARBECUE

Flank Steak Satay with Curry Dipping Sauce

Baked Tortilla Chips with Two Salsas

John's Fried Corn

John's Famous Barbecued Ribs with Secret Cure and Mango Barbecue Sauce

Roasted Potato and Fennel Salad

Green Bean and Mint Salad

Peach Pie with Oatmeal-Pecan Crust

A SOUTHWEST DINNER

Poblano Chile Dip with Baked Tortilla Chips

Country Ribs Braised with Chiles

Cinnamon Pound Cake with Mascarpone-Coffee Meringue

A CASUAL LUNCHEON

Socca

Cumin-Roasted Chicken Salad with Roasted Jalapeño Dressing

Lemon-Mascarpone Tart

AN ASIAN-INSPIRED DINNER

Tuna Tartare with Wasabi Vinaigrette

Shiitake-Dredged Salmon with Green Onion–Mushroom Compote

Mango Tart with Coconut-Macadamia Crust

Index

a

Aioli
    caper, 25
    lemongrass-soy, 10
    mint, 78–79
Apple pie, spiced hot (beverage),
    113
Apples, seared, 150
Artichokes, baked, with herb
stuffing, 138–39
Asparagus
    crab frittata, 102
    pasta with, 137
Avocados
    salad, 96–97
    salsa, 18–19

b

Babas, bourbon-soaked, 178–79
Balsamic syrup, 189
Beans. *See also* Fava beans;
    Green beans
    baked, 36
    white, and prosciutto soup, 56
Béarnaise, green peppercorn,
    94–95
Béchamel sauce, 189
Beef. *See also* New York steaks
    crown roast with pear and
        walnut dressing, 107
    flank steak, spice-rubbed,
        87–88

flank steak satay, 11
tenderloin, whole roasted,
    94–95
Bell peppers
    marinated, 46
    roasted, 186
    roasted eggplant with, 144
    rouille, 108–9
    sauce, 80–81
    –yogurt sauce, 92–93
Berries. *See also individual
        berries*
    clafoutis, mixed, 160
    summer pudding, 169
Beverages
    cocktails, 16–17, 28–29
    nonalcoholic, 112–13
    wine, 98–99
Biscuits, green onion–buttermilk,
    26
Blackberries
    compote, 164–65
    crème caramel, 154
Bok choy, sautéed baby, 34
Bourbon syrup, 178–79
Brandy-pear tart, 152–53
Brandy-vanilla syrup, 150
Brazilian, 17
Bread
    crumbs, toasted, 185–86

fava bean bruschetta, 9
green onion–buttermilk
    biscuits, 26
pudding, pumpkin, 172
salad, 39
sesame-Cheddar crackers, 22
summer pudding, 169
Broths, 71, 119
Bruschetta, fava bean, 9
Butternut squash
    gnocchi, 133–34
    sautéed, 12

c

Cakes
    chocolate volcano birthday,
        167–68
    chocolate-hazelnut torte, 161
    cinnamon pound, 170–71
    dried cherry coffee, 156
Cannelloni, pumpkin, 122–23
Carrot soup, curried, 60
Caterers, 131
Cauliflower, steamed, 42
Celeriac and fennel salad, 67
Centerpieces, 145
Cheese
    as appetizer, 40
    blue, and eggplant spread, 32
    Cheddar crackers, sesame-, 22
    eggplant lasagne, 125

Cheese, *continued*
    goat, pasta with, 137
    goat cheese salad, 57
    grilled vegetable salad, 52
    mascarpone-coffee meringue,
        170–71
    mascarpone tart, lemon-, 163
    mini pizza turnovers, 8
    passion fruit–lime cheese-
        cake, 162
    potato and tomatillo gratin,
        143
    potato napoleons, 130
    pumpkin cannelloni, 122–23
    ricotta tart, lemon-, 157
    as separate course, 40
    smoked onion–herb flan,
        140–41
    smoked salmon pizza, 30
Cheesecake, passion fruit–lime,
    162
Cherries
    coffee cake, 156
    -marinated leg of lamb,
        grilled, 84
    mixed berry clafoutis, 160
    tart, 166
Chicken
    breasts stuffed with walnut
        pesto, 76–77
    grilled honey-lemon, 115
    noodle soup, 64
    salad, cumin-roasted, 110–11
    stock, 187
Chiles
    and corn bisque, 54
    jalapeño dressing, 110–11
    poblano dip, 33
    roasted, 186
    and tomatillo salsa, 18–19
Chimichurri, 106
Chocolate
    cherry tart with, 166
    glaze, 161, 167–68
    -hazelnut torte, 161
    and macadamia nut–filled
        wontons, 151
    mousse, 175
    pecan pie with, 158
    -raspberry tart, 159
    sauce, 180

    volcano birthday cake,
        167–68
Chowder, red mussel, 62
Clafoutis, mixed berry, 160
Clams
    with hot-and-sour sauce, 38
    steamed, 114
Cocktails, 16–17, 28–29
Convection ovens, ix
Corn
    and chile bisque, 54
    fried, 37
    relish, 146–47
Corn dogs, 89
Cornish game hens, Tuscan-
    style roasted, 70
Cosmopolitan, 17
Crab
    cakes, vegetable, 108–9
    frittata, 102
Crackers, sesame-Cheddar, 22
Crème brûlée, rhubarb, 183
Crème caramel, blackberry, 154
Crème fraîche, 190
Cucumber sauce, 135–36

Eggplant
    and blue cheese spread, 32
    lasagne, 125
    roasted, 144

Fava beans
    bruschetta, 9
    spread, 9
Fennel
    and celeriac salad, 67
    and potato salad, 65
    veal stew with, 100
Fish. *See also* Salmon; Seabass;
    Tuna
    monkfish on avocado salad,
        96–97
    stock, 186–87
Flan, smoked onion–herb,
    140–41
Fries
    French, 44
    oven home, 45
Frittata, crab, 102
Fritters, vegetable, 128–29

Garlic, roasted, 185
Ginger limeade, 112
Ginger syrup, 29
Gnocchi, butternut, 133–34
Green beans
    lobster salad, 90–91
    and mint salad, 61
Green onions
    –buttermilk biscuits, 26
    –mushroom compote, 103–4

Hazelnuts
    -chocolate torte, 161
    skinned, 186
    topping, 156
Hot-and-sour sauce, 38

Lamb
    leg of, grilled cherry-
        marinated, 84
    rack of, roasted, 78–79
Lasagne, eggplant, 125
Lemon drop, 16
Lemons
    -mascarpone tart, 163
    pancakes, 176–77
Limes
    -coconut chess pie, 182
    -coconut sauce, 12
    ginger limeade, 112
    –passion fruit cheesecake,
        162
Lobster
    cooked, 186
    salad, 90–91

Macadamia and chocolate-filled
    wontons, 151
Mangoes
    barbecue sauce, 86
    Bistro mango (beverage), 113
    -ginger dipping sauce, 151
    jam, 116–17
    tart, 174
Margarita, 17
Martini, 16
Melon wedges, marinated, 14
Menus, 193–94
Monkfish on avocado salad,
    96–97

Mousse, chocolate, 175
Mushrooms
    coconut-shrimp stew, 119
    –green onion compote,
        103–4
    grilled vegetable salad, 52
    portobello soup, 66
    shiitake-dredged salmon,
        103–4
    shiitake spring rolls, 23
    soba noodles, 142
    spinach salad, 63
    stew, 126–27
    and sweet potato soufflés,
        132
    tarte Tatin, 13
Mussel chowder, red, 62

New York steaks
    with chimichurri, 106
    with olive butter, 74–75
Noodles. *See also* Pasta
    mushroom soba, 142
    orange-chile, 35
    soup, chicken, 64
Nuts, toasted, 186. *See also*
    individual nuts

Olives
    butter, 74–75
    -dressed greens, 53
    marinated, 47
    tapenade, 41
Onions
    chutney, 48–49
    –herb flan, smoked, 140–41
    smoked, 185
Orange-chile noodles, 35
Osso buco, 85
Oyster stew, 55

Pancakes
    lemon, 176–77
    potato, 15
    socca, 31
    zucchini, 146–47
Panna cotta, 164–65
Pantry, stocking, 58–59
Passion fruit
    fizzle, 113

–lime cheesecake, 162
Pasta. *See also* Noodles
    with asparagus and goat
        cheese, 137
    pumpkin cannelloni, 122–23
    seared ahi tuna on, 72–73
Pâte à choux, deep-fried
    coconut, 180
Peaches
    peeled, 189
    pie, 155
Pears
    -brandy tart, 152–53
    spice-poached, 175
    -thyme vinaigrette, 63
    and walnut dressing, 107
Pecans
    candied, 172
    -mustard dressing, 90–91
    pie, 158
Peppers. *See* Bell peppers; Chiles
Pesto
    Asian-style, 72–73
    walnut, 76–77
Pies
    lime-coconut chess, 182
    peach, 155
    pecan, 158
Pizza
    smoked salmon, 30
    turnovers, mini, 8
Planning, 82–83, 173
Pork. *See also* Prosciutto
    barbecued ribs with secret
        cure, 86
    country ribs, 101
    loin, roasted, with rosemary-
        balsamic glaze, 118
    tenderloin with spicy glaze,
        116–17
Potatoes
    best mashed, 43
    and fennel salad, 65
    French fries, 44
    napoleons, 130
    oven home fries, 45
    pancakes, 15
    roasted baby new, 41
    and tomatillo gratin, 143
Prawns. *See also* Shrimp

chile-lemongrass, 105
chilled five-spice, 25
deep-fried, with three-onion
    chutney, 48–49
Prosciutto
    fava bean bruschetta, 9
    and white bean soup, 56
Puddings
    pumpkin bread, 172
    summer, 169
Puff pastry, 190
Pumpkin
    bread pudding, 172
    cannelloni, 122–23
    –pepper bacon salad, 87–88

Raspberries
    -chocolate tart, 159
    compote, 176–77
Rhubarb crème brûlée, 183
Ribs
    barbecued, with secret cure,
        86
    country, 101
Rice
    cakes, pan-fried basmati,
        135–36
    cooked basmati, 189
    jungle, 24
    risotto with oven-roasted
        tomatoes, 124
Rouille, red pepper, 108–9

Salads
    avocado, 96–97
    bread, 39
    cumin-roasted chicken,
        110–11
    fennel and celeriac, 67
    green bean and mint, 61
    grilled vegetable, 52
    lobster, 90–91
    olive-dressed greens, 53
    oven-roasted goat cheese, 57
    pumpkin–pepper bacon,
        87–88
    roasted potato and fennel, 65
    smoked salmon, 15
    spinach, 63

Salmon
    one-minute, 10
    phyllo-wrapped, 80–81
    pizza, smoked, 30
    salad, smoked, 15
    shiitake-dredged, 103–4
Salsas
    avocado, 18–19
    tomatillo and roasted chile,
        18–19
Sauces. *See also* Aioli; Pesto;
        Salsas
    béchamel, 189
    chimichurri, 106
    chocolate, 180
    cucumber, 135–36
    curry dipping, 11
    green peppercorn béarnaise,
        94–95
    hot-and-sour, 38
    lime-coconut, 12
    mango barbecue, 86
    mango-ginger dipping, 151
    red pepper rouille, 108–9
    sage cream, 122–23
    sesame, toasted, 34
    shallot, roasted, 133–34
    sweet red pepper, 80–81
    tomato-saffron coulis,
        128–29
    yellow pepper–yogurt, 92–93
Sausage, pan-fried seafood, 20
Seabass
    pan-seared, 71
    poached, 92–93
Seafood sausage, pan-fried, 20
Secret cure, 86
Seeds, toasted, 186
Sesame seeds
    -Cheddar crackers, 22
    sauce, 34
    toasted, 186
Shallots
    fried, 185
    roasted, 185
    sauce, 133–34
    shmear, 185
Shrimp. *See also* Prawns
    -coconut stew, 119
    stock, 187–88

Simple syrup, 29
Socca, 31
Soufflés, sweet potato and
        mushroom, 132
Soups
    chicken noodle, 64
    corn and chile bisque, 54
    curried carrot, 60
    portobello mushroom, 66
    red mussel chowder, 62
    white bean and prosciutto, 56
Spices, toasted, 186
Spinach
    crab frittata, 102
    creamy garlic, 27
    eggplant lasagne, 125
    salad, 63
Spreads
    eggplant and blue cheese, 32
    fava bean, 9
Spring rolls, shiitake, 23
Squash. *See* Butternut squash;
        Pumpkin; Zucchini
Stocks, 186–88. *See also* Broths
Strawberries
    caramelized, 181
    cherry tart with, 166
Summer pudding, 169
Sweet-and-sour mix, 29
Sweet potato and mushroom
        soufflés, 132

Tapenade, olive, 41
Tarts
    brandy-pear, 152–53
    cherry, 166
    chocolate-raspberry, 159
    lemon-mascarpone, 163
    lemon-ricotta, 157
    mango, 174
    mushroom tarte Tatin, 13
    tomato-basil, 6
Tea cooler, green, 112
Tomatillos
    poblano chile dip, 33
    and potato gratin, 143
    and roasted chile salsa,
        18–19
Tomatoes, fresh
    -basil tart, 6

bread salad, 39
    mini pizza turnovers, 8
    oven-roasted, risotto
        with, 124
    peeled, 189
    roasted eggplant with, 144
    -saffron broth, 71
    -saffron coulis, 128–29
    sauce, simple, 188
    seeded, 188
Tomatoes, sundried
    osso buco with, 85
    waffles, savory, 126–27
Tortilla chips, baked, 18–19
Tuna
    seared ahi, on pasta, 72–73
    tartare, 7
Turnovers, mini pizza, 8

Veal
    osso buco, 85
    stew, 100
    stock, 187
Vegetables. *See also individual*
        vegetables
    blanched and shocked, 188
    crab cakes, 108–9
    fritters, 128–29
    salad, grilled, 52
    stock, 188

Waffles, sundried tomato,
        126–27
Walnuts
    and pear dressing, 107
    pesto, 76–77
Wine, 98–99
Wontons, chocolate and
        macadamia nut–filled, 151

Zucchini
    gratin, 21
    pancakes, 146–47